THE MAGNOLIA COLLECTION

With All Good Wishes,
Gene Westbrook

GENE WESTBROOK

To Order Additional Books:

The Magnolia Collection
P.O. Box 869
Millbrook (Montgomery), Alabama 36054

First Edition	May 1985	10,000 copies
Second Edition	June 1986	10,000 copies
Third Edition	May 1988	10,000 copies
Fourth Edition	June 1989	10,000 copies
Fifth Edition	May 1990	10,000 copies
Sixth Edition	August 1991	15,000 copies
Seventh Edition	September 1993	10,000 copies

By GENE WESTBROOK

Cover Design and Illustrations by GENIA WESTBROOK
Interior Art by GENIA WESTBROOK and JOE WESTBROOK
Editor ISABELLE HANSON PEAT
Technical Art Assistant Mark Sullivan

Printed in the USA by

FATHER&SON
ASSOCIATES, INC.
4909 North Monroe Street
Tallahassee, Florida 32303

About the Artist

Genia Westbrook is first and most importantly my daughter. She is a graduate in Visual Art and Design at Auburn University, Auburn, Alabama. This is her first endeavor in the field of book illustration and design. Her diligence and expressive talent have given the visual pleasures to this collection.

Photography

The flower photography for the artist to use for the cover illustration and other illustrations throughout the book was done by my husband, Joe Westbrook. He also contributed original artwork for the recipe pages. His photography and artwork have captured the special feelings of this collection.

Illustrations

Foreword

Dear Readers,

There must truly be something to the old expression "Southern Hospitality." We Southerners are often not even aware that this is a wonderful inborn tradition much admired by visitors from other regions. Almost invariably it leads to some form of entertaining with food. In the pages to follow are recipes for all types of entertaining with the ingredient of "Southern Hospitality" already included.

The often-asked question is "Why did you decide to write a cookbook?" By way of an attempted answer, I must tell you that this collection was accumulated as a fine old tapestry is made, by tiny threads being added through the years. I was first instructed in cooking by my mother's and grandmother's marvelous cook. Such patience with my endless questions would have put Job to shame! Then as the years have moved on, friends, friends of friends, visiting strangers, visitors from other countries, and family have been most generous with their specialities. And finally, with even more passage of time, I have added original recipes to this collection. So that in the end, this tapestry of recipes blends the tastes, travels, life-styles, and family histories of many interesting people.

Along with tapestries and "Southern Hospitality," I want to mention the long distance calls. Yes, long distance calls! From my husband's sister in Virginia — "Quick, I need a vegetable casserole. My guests are due in 15 minutes, and I burned my broccoli soufflé!" or a friend from Mississippi calling for appetizers for a party of 50 people; or my husband's mother visiting in Mobile, Alabama, — "I can't find a recipe for a blackberry cobbler anywhere; do you have one?" or a call from east Georgia for a roast recipe. Then, there's my friend from Nova Scotia who gave me a charming, red-leather-bound, blank cookbook with my name embossed in gold. I love it, but my handwriting is sad—so will this cookbook be all right instead?

With love and the hope that you will enjoy this collection,

Gene

Table of Contents

Acknowledgements

My Very Special Thanks

To my husband, Joe, and our three children, Genia, Almand, and Jay, for their enthusiastic and unfailing loyalty and love. Without you there would be no Magnolia Collection.

To my parents, Gene and Tommy Sparks. How could I possibly say "thanks" enough? I never do forget that you gave me all the right beginnings with love.

To my husband's mother, Ann Harris. All requests for help, in any endeavor, have always been more than graciously answered with love.

To Tommy Sparks, Jr., Scotty Sparks, Lucile Williams, Eloise Loeb, Mary and James Keck, Helen and Grif Carden, Dorothy and Dan Kuerner, Alice and Jack Roberts, Joan Pfeiffer, Diane and Mike Presley, Bruce and Debby Pfeiffer, Woody and Cecelia Pfeiffer. The old expression, "I couldn't have done it without you," was never more true.

To Mike and Jo Mikell, Carolyn Blackstock, and Barbara Jones for support, advice, and encouragement on many different fronts. To Hallie Head, Betsy Plummer, Nan Dessert, and John Ray for the graciously given information that assisted me in publishing this collection.

To Warren and Elizabeth Hall for giving me, as a child, my first introduction to the mountains.

To First Ladies, Nancy Reagan, Betty Ford, and Lady Bird Johnson, your recipe contributions give everyone an insight into the family life of the makers of our American history.

To all who have contributed their outstanding recipes to this collection, my simple "thanks" is from my heart.

Dawn Atkins, Mike Bannon, Rose Mary Bannon, Terry Bernstein, Carolyn Blackstock, Ken Bloch, Jackie Boggess, Tammy Bone, Shari Bozeman, Betty Burkett, Debbie Carden, Helen Carden, Nancy Leigh Douglas, Helen Doyle, Jackie Eady, Natty Elias, Betty Ford, Beth Fulghom, Lucy Glenn, Albert Gresham, Julia Mae Gresham, Leonard Gresham, Marjo Gresham, Sal Gresham, Elmore Hall, Ann Harris, Betty House, Lady Bird Johnson, Madie Keck, Mary Keck, Sylvia Kremer, Beverly Kuerner, Dorothy Kuerner, Lisa Landrum, Elise Lewis, Eloise Loeb, Georgia McKeithen, Don McLeod, Jo Mikell, Mike Mikell, Diane Morgan, Jay Payne, Bruce Pfeiffer, Cecelia Pfeiffer, Debby Pfeiffer, Joan Pfeiffer, Woody Pfeiffer, Diane Presley, Jane Quint, Nancy Reagan, Myra Reininger, Frances Roberts, Nancy Robinson, Edna Rosen, Gene Sparks, Scotty Sparks, Tom Sparks, Tommy Sparks, Jr., Pat Stevens, Mildred Sullivan, Liz Van Boeschoten, Elaine Walker, Almand Westbrook, Genia Westbrook, Jay Westbrook, Joe Westbrook, and Lucile Williams.

And grateful appreciation goes to my extraordinary friend, Isabelle Peat, for giving of her time so unstintingly in editing this collection. Extra thanks goes to her husband, David, and their children for sharing her with me during this undertaking.

All recipes have been made, tested, and enthusiastically enjoyed by my family, friends, and relatives.

Appetizers and Beverages

Crabmeat Mornay

½ cup margarine
6 tablespoons plain flour
1½ cups chicken broth
1½ cups evaporated milk
8 ounces mushrooms, drained and chopped (reserve liquid)
1 small onion, chopped
3 tablespoons pimentos, chopped

8 ounces Gruyère or Swiss cheese, grated
¼ cup Parmesan cheese, grated
1 tablespoon MSG
1 pound fresh crabmeat
⅛ teaspoon red pepper
Salt to taste

In a large skillet, melt margarine, and stir in flour until smooth. Stirring constantly, gradually add broth, keeping the sauce smooth. Add milk and mushroom liquid; then cook over medium heat, while stirring, until thickened. Stir in mushrooms, onions, pimentos, Gruyère, Parmesan, MSG, crabmeat, red pepper, and salt. Cook for another 2 minutes, while stirring. Cool and refrigerate until time to warm in a double boiler or freeze until ready to use. Serve Crabmeat Mornay in a chafing dish to keep it hot. Yield: filling for 10 dozen Timble Shells (see Appetizers).

Timble Shells

Using ready made pie pastry from the dairy case, cut rounds to fit over the outside of timble pans or mini muffin pans. Roll each pastry round with a rolling pin to make the round larger and thinner. Fit the round over the outside of each timble mold, with a little extra pastry at the top to be fluted. Prick with a fork and bake as directed on the pastry instructions. Cool slightly before removing from the pans. Allow to cool completely on paper towels. Stack very carefully, and store in airtight containers for several days, or place containers in freezer until ready to use.

Pickled Shrimp

Marinate shrimp overnight or longer.

2 pounds medium shrimp	⅓ cup vegetable oil
1 large onion, sliced in thin rings	2 drops Tabasco sauce
1 (3-ounce) bottle capers and the liquid	2 tablespoons Worcestershire sauce
⅔ cup white vinegar	Fresh dill sprig (optional)
2 bay leaves	Salt to taste

Wash shrimp in 6 changes of cold water to clean. Cook in boiling, salted water for 5 minutes or until shrimp turn pink. Allow shrimp to steep in water for 10 minutes; drain and peel the shrimp. Place shrimp in a glass or plastic container with a cover. Add onions, capers, vinegar, bay leaves, oil, Tabasco sauce, Worcestershire sauce, and dill. Mix all ingredients very gently until blended; then add salt to taste. Refrigerate covered; stir several times during the day. Drain before serving. The Pickled Shrimp will keep a week when refrigerated.

*Carefully discard the bay leaves, since the quest will be on for **shrimp** and every other goodie in the bowl. Have you ever seen a caper chased with a cocktail pick? It's quite a performance.*

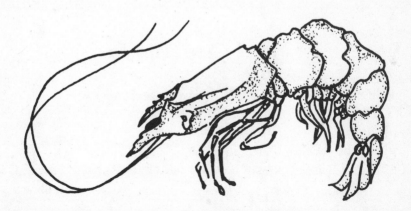

Seafood Alexandria

1	cup margarine	1	teaspoon salt
1	large clove garlic, split	¼	teaspoon pepper
1	teaspoon tarragon, crushed	1	pound raw shrimp, peeled
1	teaspoon chives, chopped	1	pound raw scallops
1	teaspoon parsley, chopped	1	pound small fresh
2	tablespoons lemon juice		mushrooms, halved

In a large skillet, melt margarine, and sauté the garlic for about 1 minute; remove and discard garlic. Add tarragon, chives, parsley, lemon juice, salt, and pepper. Turn heat to high and quickly sauté shrimp, scallops, and mushrooms until the shrimp are pink. Allow seafood to remain in the juices for 5 minutes longer. Reheat to the boiling point, and pour into a chafing dish over a low flame.

Also superb as a first course at a full dinner, or as an entrée at an informal dinner served in individual ramekins or over hot rice.

Fried Crab Claws

1   pound crab claws
Self-rising corn meal

Vegetable oil
Salt

Gently shake the crab claws in a plastic bag with corn meal to completely coat the claws. Place on a cookie sheet and put into the freezer for about 20 minutes. Fry in medium hot oil until golden brown. Drain on paper towels and lightly salt.

Serve these marvelous morsels with Quick, Great Cocktail Sauce (see Sauces) for dipping.

Scare 'Em to Death Shrimp

2 pounds fresh, large shrimp,
   heads removed, but unpeeled
1 teaspoon salt
2 tablespoons black pepper
½ pound margarine, sliced

Wash shrimp in 6 different rinses of cold water to clean. Place in a flat, glass 3-quart baking dish, sprinkle with the salt, and completely cover with the black pepper, using all of it. Place the margarine slices over the shrimp; cover and bake at 400° until the shrimp turn pink. Turn shrimp over, and bake the other side until pink. Turn oven off, and allow shrimp to remain in the hot oven for 5 minutes. Remove from the oven; stir, and allow shrimp to "rest" for 10 minutes. Serve hot.

Hot and scrumptious! A grand appetizer for the "Not-So-Faint-of-Heart."

Marvelous Crab Ring

2 hard-boiled eggs, peeled and
   sliced
2 envelopes unflavored gelatin
½ cup cold water
1 pound lump crabmeat
1 cup celery, chopped fine
2 tablespoons capers
2 cups mayonnaise
¾ cup chopped stuffed green
   olives
1 tablespoon Worcestershire
   sauce
2 tablespoons lemon juice
Dash of sugar
Coarse black pepper to taste
5 drops Tabasco (more if
   desired)
1 teaspoon onion juice

Grease a 5½ cup ring mold with vegetable oil, and arrange egg slices in the bottom of the mold. Use only the slices with the yolk showing to line mold. Chop any remaining egg, and add as a final ingredient. Soak gelatin in the water for 15 minutes. Place gelatin mixture over a bowl of hot water, and stir to dissolve. Set aside. Combine all remaining ingredients; mix well. Add dissolved gelatin to the crab mixture; mix very carefully, and pour into the ring mold. Cover and refrigerate until ring is well set. Unmold just before serving, and garnish. Yield: 5½ cup ring.

Shari's Salmon Roll

1	pound can salmon, drained	3	tablespoons onion, minced
8	ounces cream cheese, softened	½	cup pecans, chopped
1	tablespoon lemon juice	3	tablespoons fresh parsley, minced
¼	teaspoon salt		

After draining the salmon, remove all skin and bones hidden inside. Combine salmon that has been flaked, cream cheese, lemon juice, salt, and onion. Mix until well blended. Cover and refrigerate for several hours. Form into logs, a ball, or be creative and form a whole salmon (will need to double recipe). If using logs or a ball, mix pecans and parsley, and roll to coat outside. If making the salmon, stir pecans into mixture and forget the parsley. Refrigerate to store, or freeze. Serve with Homemade Melba Toast (see Appetizers).

Once for a party, my very talented husband "sculpted" a whole salmon. Its head and tail were raised with cucumber "scales", lemon slice "fins", olive "eyes", etc. Nothing short of spectacular, I thought, until a little 'ole lady toddled by the table and commented on the "adorable dragon!"

Homemade Melba Toast for Appetizers

1   loaf very thin white bread

Cut crusts from the loaf with an electric knife; then cut loaf both lengthwise and crosswise making 4 squares from each slice of bread. Place squares on cookie sheets, and bake at 250° until light brown. Store in an airtight container.

These are a welcomed change from the usual crackers served. If you'd like to add something extra, spread garlic butter on the slices before cutting into squares, and sprinkle with Parmesan cheese.

Shrimp Dainties

1 pound fresh shrimp, cleaned
  and cooked
1 tablespoon onion, minced
1 teaspoon celery, minced
1 teaspoon green pepper,
  minced
2 teaspoons grated lemon rind

¼ teaspoon salt
1-3 drops Tabasco sauce
Dash of pepper
¾ cup mayonnaise
36 bread rounds, half-dollar size
Paprika

Cut shrimp into very fine pieces; mix with onion, celery, green pepper, lemon rind, salt, Tabasco sauce, pepper, and mayonnaise. Pile a heaping teaspoon of shrimp mixture on each bread round, and garnish with a little paprika. Refrigerate and serve cold. Yield: 36.

Petite Shrimp Pastries

Filling:
1 small onion, minced
½ pound mushrooms, chopped
1 pound raw shrimp, peeled
  and coarsely chopped into 4
  pieces per shrimp

3 tablespoons margarine,
  melted
1 teaspoon salt
1 drop Tabasco sauce
2 tablespoons plain flour
¼ cup sour cream

Pastry:
9 ounces cream cheese,
  softened

½ cup margarine
1½ cups plain flour

To prepare filling, sauté onions, mushrooms, and shrimp pieces in the melted margarine until shrimp are pink. Add salt, Tabasco sauce, flour, and sour cream; mix well. Cover and chill until cold.
To prepare pastry, blend all pastry ingredients in food processor until a dough forms. Wrap the dough in waxed paper, and chill. To make the pastries, roll chilled dough on a floured surface until thin. Cut out circles, and place small amount of cold shrimp filling to one side of the circle. Fold circle in half; seal the edge with a fork. Place on a cookie sheet and bake in a preheated oven at 400° for about 12 minutes or until lightly browned on top. Yield: 45.

Shrimp Cheese Puffs

½ cup margarine, softened
2 cups sharp Cheddar cheese, grated
1 egg yolk
1 egg white, stiffly beaten

30 bread squares (4 quarters per slice of bread)
30 medium size boiled shrimp, peeled
Paprika

Cream margarine and cheese; then blend in egg yolk, and fold in egg white. Arrange bread squares on a greased cookie sheet and top each square with a boiled shrimp. Top each shrimp with a rounded teaspoon of the cheese mixture; sprinkle with paprika.. Bake at 350° until bread is slightly browned and crisp. Yield: 30.

Chimichangas

1 dozen frozen flour tortillas
1 cup tomato sauce
1 cup cooked sausage or ground beef
1 small onion, chopped
½ teaspoon chili powder

½ teaspoon garlic powder
¼ teaspoon cocoa (do not omit)
¼ teaspoon cumin powder
Pinch of sugar
Salt to taste
Vegetable oil for frying

Allow tortillas to thaw while preparing the meat filling. In a saucepan, combine tomato sauce, cooked meat, onion, chili powder, garlic powder, cocoa, cumin, sugar, and salt. Bring to a boil, cover, and reduce heat to simmer for 10 minutes. Allow filling to cool. Lay the tortillas on a clean surface, and divide the filling evenly in the center of each tortilla. Fold each tortilla like an envelope, and secure with a toothpick. Deep fry on medium heat until golden brown. Drain on paper towel, and keep warm, uncovered, on a warming tray until ready to serve. Yield: 12.

Was serving Chimichangas one evening during the testing process for this book, when a guest reached for his fourth Chimichanga and commented, "Don't know what these are called, but they're a definite 'go' for the book." I took his advice.

Down East Clams in the Shell

4 (7½-ounce) cans clams	½ teaspoon Worcestershire sauce
8 tablespoons margarine	2 teaspoons lemon juice
2 cups Italian bread crumbs	2 cups clam juice, divided
1 teaspoon basil	Clam shells, half dollar size
1 teaspoon thyme	Parmesan cheese, grated
1 teaspoon marjoram	Paprika

Drain clams, reserving the liquid; chop the clams. Mix melted margarine, bread crumbs, basil, thyme, marjoram, Worcestershire, lemon, and clams; then add enough clam juice to make mixture spreadable. Fill well-cleaned clam shells with mixture. Sprinkle with Parmesan cheese and paprika; then dot with margarine. Bake at 350° for 20-25 minutes. Serve with a cocktail fork.

The shells add a very "salty" touch to a party. They don't have to be exotic, just ones picked up on a long walk along a beach watching the sun sink into the ocean.

Chinese Pick-Up Sticks

3 tablespoons margarine	1 (3-ounce) can chow mein noodles
2 teaspoons soy sauce	¼ teaspoon celery salt
2-4 drops Tabasco sauce	Scant ⅛ teaspoon onion powder

In a small saucepan, melt margarine; add soy sauce and Tabasco sauce. Mix well. Place noodles in a bowl, and drizzle sauce over them; toss to coat the noodles. Sprinkle with celery salt and onion powder; toss again. Spread noodles on a cookie sheet. Bake at 275° until lightly browned. Yield: 2½ cups.

Crab-Stuffed Mushrooms

8 ounces cream cheese, softened
1 tablespoon milk
6½ ounces canned crab meat
2 tablespoons green onion, minced
½ teaspoon horseradish

Dash of Worcestershire sauce
Salt to taste
Tabasco sauce to taste
25 fresh mushrooms, washed and stems removed
Very fine cracker crumbs

In a bowl, combine cream cheese, milk, crab, green onion, horseradish, Worcestershire sauce, salt, and Tabasco sauce; mix very well. Dry the mushrooms, and salt on all sides. Fill mushroom caps with the crab mixture, and place in a greased baking dish. Sprinkle tops with the cracker crumbs, and bake at 350° for about 10 minutes or until crab stuffing is bubbling. Yield: 25 mushrooms.

London Towns

½ pound bacon, fried slowly until very crisp
1 pound sharp Cheddar cheese, grated

1 large onion, minced very fine
1 tablespoon Worcestershire sauce
1 loaf party rye, sliced

Place bacon, cheese, onion, and Worcestershire sauce into a blender or food processor; blend into a spread. Place spread on rye slices, and broil until brown and bubbling. Yield: about 30.

Jackie's Chalupa Grande

3 (10½-ounce) cans jalapeño bean dip
1 pound ground beef, cooked and drained
1 (1⅛-ounce) package taco mix
1 (4-ounce) can chopped green chilies
2 ripe avocados, peeled and pitted
4 tablespoons sour cream
3 tablespoons lemon juice
Salt to taste
5 green onions, chopped
1 cup black olives, chopped
1 green pepper, chopped
4 tomatoes, diced
1½ cups sharp Cheddar cheese
1½ cups Monterey Jack cheese
Alfalfa sprouts (optional)

Mix bean dip, ground beef, taco mix, and green chilies until well blended. Spread this mixture in a layer onto a large attractive platter with a small lip. In the food processor or blender, puree the avocado; then mix in the sour cream, lemon juice, and salt to taste. Layer the bean and beef mixture with the avocado mixture. Mix green onions, black olives, green peppers, and diced tomatoes, and sprinkle over the avocado layer. In a food processor or Mouli grater, finely grate the two cheeses together. This mixes the cheeses for a special effect. Sprinkle cheeses over the top to cover. Alfalfa sprouts are the final layer, if desired. Serve with tortilla chips. Serves a crowd!

Spectacular hors d'oeuvre! It's very colorful and appealing. Sometimes I reverse layers of vegetables and cheeses and leave off the alfalfa sprouts. Place cheeses on the avocado layer. Do not mix vegetables, instead make concentric circles of the tomatoes, green peppers, black olives, green onions, and a small mound of tomatoes in the center.

Skewered Pork and Pineapple Tidbits

The pork requires overnight marination.

2   pounds lean pork
2 or 3 cans (20-ounce) pineapple
  chunks, reserve liquid
1   large garlic clove, crushed
1½ cups soy sauce

¼   cup cooking sherry
1   teaspoon ground ginger
Wooden skewers soaked in
  water for 1 hour before using

Trim all excess fat from the pork, and cut into cubes the proper size to thread onto wooden skewers. In a flat glass baking dish, mix the pineapple liquid, garlic, soy sauce, sherry, and ginger. Add cubed pork and pineapple chunks; stir to coat all pieces. Cover and refrigerate overnight; stir occasionally to allow even marinating. When ready to serve, thread pork cubes and pineapple chunks onto the skewers, and grill over hot coals until pork is thoroughly cooked. Serve on the skewers.

Elmore's Spicy Spinach Dip

1   (10-ounce) package frozen
  chopped spinach
8   ounces mayonnaise
1   envelope Knorr vegetable
  soup mix

8   ounces sour cream
1   (8½-ounce) can water
  chestnuts, chopped
½   small onion, minced

Thaw spinach completely; then squeeze all the water out. Mix spinach with the other ingredients; blend well. Refrigerate overnight before serving. Serve on crisp crackers or with chips.

Beef Empanadas

12 ounces lean ground beef	1½ teaspoons cornstarch
1 cup onion, minced	1 teaspoon salt
1 cup green pepper, minced	1 teaspoon sugar
1 cup chopped tomato	½ teaspoon black pepper
1 clove garlic, minced	2 to 3 drops Tabasco sauce

Pastry:

3 cups unsifted plain flour	¾ cup vegetable oil
1 teaspoon salt	½ cup water
1 teaspoon baking powder	

Preheat oven to 425° about 15 minutes before baking time. In a skillet, brown beef and drain. Add onion, green pepper, tomato, and garlic; cook for about 10 minutes or until onion is transparent. Stir in cornstarch, salt, sugar, pepper, and Tabasco sauce. Continue cooking, while stirring, for 5 minutes. Remove from heat, and allow to cool while making the pastry. In a medium bowl, mix flour, salt, and baking powder. Combine oil and water; then add to flour mixture. Stir until a soft dough forms. Divide into 22 balls; then roll each ball between two sheets of waxed paper into a flat circle. Place a heaping tablespoon of beef mixture in the center of each circle. Fold circle in half, and seal the edges with the tines of a fork. Place empanadas on ungreased cookie sheet, and bake at 425° for 10 to 15 minutes or until lightly browned. Serve hot or cold. Yield: 22.

The longer the preparation time for an appetizer, the quicker it goes at a party. I've seen some "store-bought" dips last longer than Rip Van Winkle slept! Bite the bullet, and make this recipe at least double. These Empanadas definitely will not languish on the cocktail table.

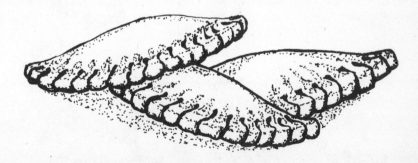

Won Tons

4 slices bacon	½ teaspoon ground ginger
½ pound ground beef	Soy sauce to taste
½ large cabbage, shredded very fine	1 package won ton skins
2 large onions, sliced in thin rings	Dry white wine
	Extra soy sauce for the dipping sauce

In a skillet or wok, fry bacon until crisp, and remove to drain; reserve the bacon drippings. In another skillet, cook ground beef, and drain; then crumble the beef and the bacon. Add the cabbage and onions to the skillet with bacon drippings and cook over medium heat for 2 minutes. Stir in the beef, bacon, and ginger; cook over medium heat for 2 minutes. Stir and add soy sauce to taste. Continue cooking and stirring until the cabbage is very wilted and soft. Put water in a small, open bowl; then dip all edges of won ton skin into the water. When edges are dampened, place a small amount of cabbage filling in the center of the won ton skin; then fold over into a triangle shape and carefully seal the dampened edges by pressing with the fingers. Continue to make won tons until all filling is used. In an electric skillet, heat vegetable oil to hot, but not smoking; then reduce heat to medium-high, and fry the won tons until golden brown, turning once. Drain very well on paper towel. Do not stack or cover. To keep warm until serving time, place on fresh paper-towel-covered cookie sheets, uncovered, on a warming tray. Serve Won Tons with a bowl of 1 part dry white wine to 3 parts soy sauce for dipping. Use small plates for the Won Tons, since the soy mixture is messy and stains.

An absolutely endless supply of Won Tons can be eaten at a party, not to mention the depletion from roving Won Ton thieves in the kitchen. Perhaps, you might consider a Chinese chef and an armed guard to get them to the table!

Marinated "Yak"

Marinate overnight.

2½ pounds round steak
½ cup vegetable oil
1 cup soy sauce
½ cup vinegar
2 medium purple onions, cut in pieces large enough to be skewered

2 large celery ribs, cut in pieces large enough to be skewered
2 tablespoons coarse ground black pepper

Trim the beef of any fat; cut into bite-size pieces. In a skillet, heat oil on high, and stir-fry the beef, a small amount at a time, until all beef is browned and seared. Pour the beef and all juices into a glass bowl. Add soy sauce, vinegar, onions, celery, and pepper; mix well. Cover and refrigerate overnight; stir occasionally. Serve undrained and cold, using long wooden skewers or cocktail picks for skewering.

Of course, the meat is beef, not yak. The title just makes interesting cocktail conversation.

Sausage and Cheese-Stuffed Mushrooms

24 large fresh mushrooms
Salt
¾ pound lean pork sausage
¼ teaspoon garlic powder

2 tablespoons parsley, chopped
1 cup sharp Cheddar cheese, grated

Preheat oven to 350°. Rinse mushrooms, and pat dry; remove the stems. Salt mushroom caps all over. Chop stems; then add sausage, garlic powder, and parsley. Cook mixture until sausage is well done; then drain off all grease, and crumble. Stir in the cheese; mix well. Spoon mixture into mushroom caps, and place in a 9×13-inch greased baking dish. Bake at 350° for 20 minutes. Yield: 2 dozen.

Jo's Mini-Pizzas

1 pound mild sausage	1 teaspoon garlic salt
1 pound hot sausage	1 pound Velveeta cheese, cubed
1 cup onion, chopped	
½ medium green pepper, chopped	1 pound Mozzarella cheese, cubed
1 tablespoon oregano	3 loaves party rye bread, sliced
1 tablespoon fennel seeds (can be omitted)	

Preheat oven to 425° about 15 minutes before cooking time. In a large, non-stick skillet, cook both sausages, onion, and green pepper until sausage is browned. Drain well on absorbent paper towel. Return sausage to skillet; add oregano, fennel seeds, and garlic salt. Stir and add both cheeses. Place over low heat, and gently stir mixture while cheeses melt; then remove from the heat. Spread a scant tablespoon of mixture on each slice of rye bread. Place rye slices on cookie sheets, and bake at 425° for 8 to 10 minutes. If preparing ahead of time, place rye slices, with the mixture on them, on the cookie sheet and freeze. When frozen, remove to a Ziploc bag, and keep frozen until ready to bake.

Broccoli Balls

1 (10-ounce) package frozen broccoli, cut pieces or spears	Salt and pepper to taste
1 small onion, minced	1 egg yolk
1 tablespoon margarine	Ritz cracker crumbs

Cook broccoli in salted boiling water until very tender, and drain completely. In the food processor, chop onion; then add drained broccoli, and process for 2 seconds. Remove from food processor into a skillet with the margarine melted, and sauté for 5 minutes. Add salt and pepper. Let mixture cool; then add the egg yolk, and mix well. Form into small balls about teaspoon size, and roll in the cracker crumbs. Fry in preheated oil until light brown. Drain well on paper towels. Yield: about 50.

Far East Cocktail Rings

⅓ package Sai Fun noodles
Hot water
1 pound ground beef, cooked and drained
½ package (10-ounce) frozen peas and carrots, thawed

1 medium onion, minced
1 egg, well beaten
½ teaspoon MSG
Salt and pepper to taste
3 cans refrigerated crescent dinner rolls

Preheat oven according to roll package instructions. Soak Sai Fun noodles in hot water until soft. Drain, and cut noodles into 1-inch lengths. Combine ground beef, uncooked peas and carrots, onions, noodles, and egg; mix well. Add MSG, then salt and pepper to taste. This mixture is the stuffing for the rolls. Open rolls, and divide into **only four** rolls per can. Seal the perforated diagonal cut. Fill rolls with stuffing; roll and seal seam and ends very thoroughly. Bake in a preheated oven according to the roll package instructions. Add a little extra cooking time, but watch very closely not to burn. Allow rolls to cool; then slice with an electric knife, and serve.

Buy the Sai Fun noodles in an Oriental food market, and give it a go. Not difficult to make, just a little something unusual.

Sausalito Chili Dip

1 pound ground beef
2 tablespoons catsup
1½ cups sharp Cheddar cheese, grated
½ cup onion, minced

½ cup stuffed olives, halved
1 teaspoon chili powder
Jalapeño relish to taste
1 (15-ounce) can kidney beans, drained and mashed

In a large skillet, cook ground beef until browned; drain. Add all other ingredients, and cook slowly until cheese is melted. Serve in a chafing dish, fondue pot, etc. to keep warm. Use tortilla chips for dipping.

The jalapeño relish is the key ingredient. Don't go wild, but do give it a good hot zip.

Bruce's Nachos

For microwave or oven.

16 ounces round tortilla chips
1 (10½-ounce) can bean dip
8 ounces Monterey Jack cheese, grated
8 ounces sharp Cheddar cheese, grated

Hot taco sauce
1 bunch green onions, chopped
1 jar Hormel real bacon bits
Seasoned salt
Jalapeño peppers, sliced

In a 3-quart glass baking dish, arrange tortilla chips, and spread with a thin layer of bean dip. Add both types cheese, taco sauce, onions, bacon bits, a small sprinkle of seasoned salt, and top with a jalapeño pepper slice. Microwave on high just long enough for the cheese to melt, or heat in the oven until cheese melts.

A great variation is a layer of sour cream on top of the layer of bean dip. Make plenty of these, since they will quickly disappear!

Beef Logs

2 pounds lean ground beef
1 teaspoon mustard seed
2 tablespoons Worcestershire sauce
2 tablespoons coarse ground black pepper

½ teaspoon garlic powder
1 teaspoon onion flakes
3 tablespoons seasoned salt
Paprika, sprinkled on outside of logs before cooking

Blend all ingredients thoroughly; then form into 3 "logs." Refrigerate for 24 hours; then wrap in foil, and punch 4 holes in bottom of foil. Place on a pan with a rack to allow fat to drain out. Bake at 325° for about 1 hour. Unwrap to cool. Wrap in plastic and store in a Ziploc bag in the refrigerator or freezer. When ready to serve, slice thin and serve with crackers.

The Beef Logs are hot and spicy. They can even be served like sausage at a brunch or for breakfast.

Skewered Beef Appetizers

Marinate overnight, if possible.

1 pound round steak, 1 inch
thick
2 tablespoons sherry
⅓ cup soy sauce
Wooden skewers for beef strips

1 clove garlic, crushed
½ teaspoon sugar
1 (1-inch) piece thinly sliced
fresh ginger, or ½ teaspoon
ground ginger

Trim all fat from the meat; then place meat in the freezer, and partially freeze for easier slicing. While beef is cooling, mix all other ingredients until well blended. Slice the partially frozen beef into thin slices, and marinate for at least one hour, overnight is better. While beef is marinating, soak the wooden skewers in water for 1 hour to prevent scorching. Thread beef strips onto the skewers, and grill over hot coals until beef is done.

Stuffed Mushrooms

24 large mushrooms
Salt
1 cup cooked sausage, drained
and crumbled
1 cup mushroom stems,
minced
3 tablespoons margarine,
melted

1 medium onion, minced
1 small clove garlic, minced
2 tablespoons sour cream
½ cup fine Italian bread
crumbs
½ cup Parmesan cheese, grated
Paprika

Wash mushrooms, and remove stems. Allow mushrooms to dry while chopping the stems very fine. Salt mushrooms all over including the inside of the caps, and place on a greased baking pan. Combine the sausage, mushroom stems, margarine, onion, garlic, sour cream, bread crumbs, and Parmesan cheese; mix well. Stuff the mushroom caps; then sprinkle with paprika, and bake at 350° for 25 minutes. Yield: 24.

Debby's Tex Mex Strata

3 medium ripe avocados,
   peeled and pitted
4 tablespoons lemon juice
½ teaspoon salt or more to
   taste
4 drops Tabasco sauce
¼ teaspoon pepper
8 ounces sour cream
½ cup mayonnaise
1 (1¼-ounce) package taco
   seasoning mix
2 (10½-ounce) cans jalapeño
   bean dip

1 large bunch green onions,
   chopped
3 medium size tomatoes,
   seeded and coarsely chopped
2 (3½-ounce) cans pitted ripe
   olives, drained and coarsely
   chopped
16 ounces sharp Cheddar
   cheese, grated
Round tortilla chips

In a medium-size bowl, mash avocados; add lemon juice, salt, Tabasco sauce, and pepper. In another bowl, combine sour cream, mayonnaise, and taco mix. In a 9×13 inch glass casserole, spread the bean dip in a layer. Next, spread the avocado mixture; then the sour cream mixture. Sprinkle with the green onions, chopped tomatoes, chopped olives; then cover top with the cheese. Refrigerate until serving time. Use tortilla chips for dipping.

Can be prepared in advance through the sour cream layer, and refrigerated. Add remaining layers at serving time.

Pat's East Texas Chili Dip

1   (15-ounce) can chili without
    beans
1   pound Velveeta cheese, cut
    into pieces

5   green onions, chopped
    Tortilla rounds for dipping

Place the chili and cheese pieces in an ovenproof dish. Top with the green onions, and bake at 350° until cheese is melted and bubbling. Mix the cheese and chili to blend. Pour into a chafing dish to keep dip warm during serving time. Serve with tortilla rounds.

Especially good to serve in the winter since this dip is very hearty. We also enjoy it for "Sunday Surprise." At our house, Sunday night supper can bring many surprises—usually that everyone has to "fend for himself" in the refrigerator! So quickly put this dip together, and serve in a bowl over broken tortilla chips, and "Sunday Surprise" will turn out to be a treat.

Hot Sausage Balls

1½ cups plain flour
¼   teaspoon salt
1   teaspoon paprika

8   ounces sharp Cheddar
    cheese, grated
¼   cup margarine
1   pound hot sausage

There are 2 methods for preparing the sausage balls. Preheat oven to 400° about 15 minutes before cooking time.
Method 1, mix all ingredients; then form into balls. Bake at 400° until balls are light brown. Remove from oven and drain on paper towel. This is the quickest method.
Method 2, mix flour, salt, paprika, cheese, and margarine into a dough. Form balls with the sausage; then cover with the dough. Bake at 400° until light brown. Remove from oven, and drain on paper towel.

Both variations are delicious, although they taste different. The balls can be made ahead of time and frozen. Use them all at once for a party, or bake a few at a time to serve when the mood strikes.

Beth's Hors D'Oeuvre Cheese Pastry

2½ cups plain flour, sifted
1 cup margarine
1 cup sour cream
Seasoned salt

3 cups grated sharp Cheddar
    cheese, divided
Paprika

Preheat oven to 350° about 15 minutes before baking time. In an electric mixer, cream flour, margarine, and sour cream into a dough. Divide into 4 balls, and chill. After chilling, roll each ball into a 6×12-inch rectangle. Sprinkle each rectangle with a light cover of seasoned salt, and ¾ cup of the cheese. Roll jellyroll style, beginning on the long edge. Pinch ends together, and place on a greased cookie sheet. Partially cut through the roll at 1-inch intervals, but do not cut completely through. Sprinkle with paprika. Bake in a preheated oven at 350° for 30 minutes.

This very delicate pastry will serve for almost any occasion, including breakfast.

Carolyn's Cheesy Jalapeño Squares

1 (4-ounce) can jalapeños,
    chopped
6 eggs, beaten well

1 pound sharp Cheddar
    cheese, grated

Grease a 2-quart baking dish, and make a layer of the chopped jalapeños. Sprinkle cheese over the peppers; then pour beaten eggs evenly over the cheese. Bake at 350° for 1 hour. Cool slightly; then cut into squares.

Marinated Black Olives and Cherry Tomatoes

Prepare at least one day in advance.

1 cup vegetable oil	1 teaspoon oregano
1 cup cider vinegar	1 medium clove garlic, minced
2 teaspoons salt	1 pint cherry tomatoes
¼ teaspoon sugar	2 (16-ounce) cans pitted black olives, drained
1 teaspoon cracked black pepper	

In a medium bowl, mix oil, vinegar, salt, sugar, pepper, oregano, and garlic until well blended. Divide marinade into 2 bowls. Pierce each tomato with a fork once, and add to 1 of the bowls with the marinade. Add drained olives to the other bowl with marinade. Cover and refrigerate. Stir during the day several times to assure all ingredients are marinating. Before serving, drain marinade. Yield: 4 cups.

For a truly stunning appetizer, marinate mushroom caps and large, stuffed green olives in the marinade with the tomatoes. Serve in a crystal bowl to set off the glistening colors.

Pickled Mushrooms

Prepare at least one day in advance of serving.

4 (6-ounce) cans button mushrooms	2 teaspoons salt
4 tablespoons vegetable oil	2 cloves garlic, minced
½ cup white vinegar	½ teaspoon oregano

Drain mushrooms; mix oil, vinegar, salt, garlic, and oregano in a large jar. Cap tightly, and shake vigorously until well mixed; add mushrooms, and gently mix. Cap jar and refrigerate. Mushrooms keep in the refrigerator quite a long time. Serve mushrooms drained, and room temperature.

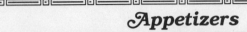

Cheese Straws

8   ounces New York State
    sharp Cheddar cheese,
    grated

½   cup margarine
1½ cups plain flour, sifted
Cayenne pepper to taste

Preheat oven to 350°
Allow cheese and margarine to come to room temperature in a mixer bowl. In an electric mixer, cream the cheese and margarine. Add flour and cayenne pepper, mixing to form a soft dough. If dough is too sticky, add 1 or 2 more tablespoons flour. Form dough into rolls to fit a cookie press with the ridged line opening in place. Press straws from the cookie press onto a greased cookie sheet. Cut into 3-inch sections. Bake in preheated oven at 350° on the middle rack of the oven for about 15 minutes. Cheese straws should not brown on top. Watch carefully since they cook quickly.

The cayenne pepper gives this recipe its zip; do not leave it out. Perfect to keep frozen to use on spur of the moment occasions.

Cheese Puffs

For a good laugh about how times have changed, check the prices.

1   stick butter
40 cents N.Y. State cheese
3   buttons of garlic

40 cents mild cheese
4 or 5 tablespoons mayonnaise

Found this in an old file. Wonder how old it is?

Two Way Salsa — for Gringos or Mexicans

Canned jalapeño pepper, minced
  (optional)
½ medium onion, minced
2 tablespoons vegetable oil
½ teaspoon salt
1 (4½-ounce) can chopped
  black olives
4 ounces green olives, chopped
4 tablespoons vinegar
3 large tomatoes, chopped

For Gringos:
Mix all ingredients **except** jalapeños. Cover and refrigerate for at least 1 hour before serving. Serve with tortilla chips.

For Mexicans:
Mix all ingredients including all the jalapeño peppers you are brave enough to use. Actually, a small amount of jalapeño makes a delightful salsa which isn't life threatening. Cover and refrigerate for at least 1 hour before serving. Serve with tortilla chips and a fan.

Cheese Wafers

1 cup margarine
4 cups sharp Cheddar cheese,
  grated
2 cups plain flour
1 teaspoon red pepper
2 cups nuts, finely chopped
1 teaspoon salt (if needed)
2 cups Rice Krispies

Preheat oven to 300° about 15 minutes before baking time. In an electric mixer, cream margarine and cheese; then add flour, red pepper, nuts, and salt; blend well. Stir the Rice Krispies in by hand. Divide into 5 pieces, and roll into logs about the diameter of a 50¢ piece. Chill logs in refrigerator or freezer until very firm or lightly frozen. Slice ¼ inch thick with an electric knife. Bake on a greased cookie sheet at 300° for about 15 to 20 minutes. Yield: about 165.

The logs can be frozen before cooking, or the wafers can be frozen after cooking. Cooked wafers also can be stored in airtight containers. Very handy to have made for impromptu occasions. They also make grand gifts for friends who like goodies with a hot and nippy flavor.

Hot Cheese Squares

1 jar Old English sharp cheese	½ teaspoon red pepper
8 ounces sharp Cheddar cheese, grated	1 tablespoon Worcestershire sauce
½ cup margarine, softened	4 slices white bread
1 tablespoon mayonnaise	Paprika
½ teaspoon salt	

Bring both cheeses and margarine to room temperature. Using an electric mixer or food processor, blend cheeses, margarine, mayonnaise, salt, red pepper, and Worcestershire sauce. Stack the 4 slices of bread on top of each other, and trim the crusts with an electric knife. "Ice" the sides of the stacked bread with the cheese mixture; then cut into 4 squares completely through the stack to produce 16 squares. Spread the top surface of each square with cheese mixture, and arrange on a cookie sheet. Sprinkle with paprika, and bake at 350° for 10 minutes or until cheese is very warm but not melted. The squares can be frozen in Ziploc bags until ready to bake. Yield: 16 squares.

Hot Artichoke Appetizer

1 (14-ounce) can artichoke hearts, drained and chopped	1 cup Parmesan cheese, grated
½ teaspoon garlic powder	1 cup mayonnaise
8 ounces cream cheese	¼ teaspoon Worcestershire sauce

Mix all ingredients well; then spoon into a lightly greased baking dish. Bake at 350° for 20-30 minutes. Serve with Homemade Melba Toast (see Appetizers). Yield: 3 cups.

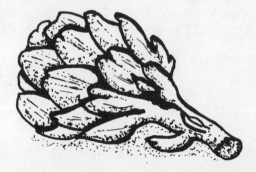

Mushrooms Marseilles

2 pounds small fresh mushrooms	Coarse ground pepper to taste
1 cup butter	¼ teaspoon nutmeg
¼ cup fresh parsley, chopped	Salt to taste
4 cloves garlic, crushed	1 loaf very fresh French bread, cut in cubes for dipping

Cut stems of mushrooms off near the caps, and wash thoroughly; drain. In a skillet, melt butter, and add parsley, garlic, pepper, and nutmeg. Bring butter mixture to a boil; add mushrooms, and reduce heat to simmer. Cook, stirring, for about 10 minutes. Salt to taste. Pour mushrooms and butter sauce into a chafing dish over a low flame. Serve with fondue forks or long wooden skewers for skewering mushrooms and dipping bread cubes in the sauce.

Ha' Pennies

½ cup margarine	½ package dry onion soup mix
8 ounces sharp Cheddar cheese, grated	1 cup plain flour
	¾ cup pecans, chopped fine

Preheat oven to 375° about 15 minutes before cooking time. Bring margarine and cheese to room temperature; then cream. Add onion soup mix, flour, and pecans to form a stiff dough. Roll into logs about 1 inch in diameter. Wrap in waxed paper, and chill in refrigerator or freezer. When chilled, slice ¼ inch thick, using an electric knife. Bake at 375° for 10-15 minutes or until very light brown. Cool and store in the freezer or in an airtight container.

These make great appetizers for a party or very welcomed gifts delivered in a pretty tin.

Almond Pinecones

1¼ pounds whole blanched almonds
8 ounces cream cheese, softened
¼ cup mayonnaise
¼ cup Pickapepper sauce
6 slices bacon, cooked very crisp and crumbled
2 tablespoons green onion, chopped
½ teaspoon cracked black pepper

Preheat oven to 300°. Spread almonds in a single layer on a cookie sheet; bake for about 15 minutes, stirring often, until almonds just begin to color brown. Mix together cream cheese, mayonnaise, and Pickapepper sauce until well blended. Add bacon, onions, and pepper; mix well. Cover and refrigerate overnight. Form the cheese mixture into the shape of two pinecones on an attractive serving platter. Beginning at the narrow end, press almonds at a slight angle into cheese mixture in rows that overlap. Continue overlapping rows until all cheese is covered. Refrigerate until serving time. Garnish with articifial pine sprigs. Serve with crackers or Homemade Melba Toast (see Appetizers). Yield: 1½ cups.

Gorgeous on your hors d'oeuvre table, not to mention that it tastes grand, too.

Eloise's Cocktail Cucumbers

Make one day in advance.

½ cup sugar
½ cup white vinegar
¼ cup water
1 teaspoon salt
1 teaspoon dill weed
2 medium unpeeled cucumbers, sliced thin

Bring to a boil in a saucepan the sugar, vinegar, water, salt, and dill weed. Mix to dissolve and blend. Place cucumbers in a glass bowl, and pour the hot marinade over them. Cover, and refrigerate overnight. Drain before serving.

Marinated Carrots

Marinate overnight before serving.

8 large carrots, peeled and cut into julienne strips	2 cloves garlic, peeled and split
Boiling water	1 teaspoon dried thyme
½ cup vegetable oil	Juice of 1 lemon
½ cup white vinegar	⅛ teaspoon pepper
1 small onion, sliced thin	Salt to taste

Cover carrot strips with boiling water in a saucepan; place lid on pan and cook. Stir several times during cooking. Remove from heat when carrots are barely tender; drain. Combine oil, vinegar, onion, garlic, thyme, lemon juice, and pepper. Place drained carrots in a glass bowl, and pour marinade over them. Toss very gently to coat; then cover and refrigerate. Stir occasionally, and check once for salt. Keep refrigerated overnight. Drain before serving. Carrots will keep refrigerated for several days.

Traditionally, carrots are not usually a sought-after item on an hors d'oeuvre table. Somehow, these slip the surly bonds of the ordinary and actually are requested again. Amazing!

Blue and Chili Dip

4 ounces blue cheese	Chili sauce

Soften blue cheese; then stir in the chili sauce to individual taste. Refrigerate for several hours before serving. Spread on Homemade Melba Toast (See Appetizers). Keep refrigerated to store.

"Gift Wrapped" Cheese Box

1 pound New York State sharp Cheddar cheese, grated	2 tablespoons minced onion flakes
2 (3-ounce) packages cream cheese, softened	1 cup walnuts, minced
¼ teaspoon garlic powder	1 tablespoon chili powder
1 tablespoon Worcestershire sauce	Whole pimentos
	Stuffed green olive slices

In an electric mixer, cream Cheddar cheese and cream cheese. Add garlic powder, Worcestershire sauce, onion flakes, and walnuts. Mix thoroughly, and refrigerate until cold. Form cheese mixture into a square box, and evenly coat with the chili powder. Slice the whole pimentos into long strips. Use the strips of pimento like a ribbon to tie a bow around the box. Garnish with the olive slices. Store in the refrigerator.

Diane's Delectable Dip with Hawaiian Bread

2 tablespoons vinegar	½ small carrot, peeled
½ cup cottage cheese	½ small onion
1 cup mayonnaise	¼ green pepper
¼ teaspoon salt	1 loaf Hawaiian bread (round)
¼ teaspoon curry powder	Vegetable sticks

Place all ingredients into a food processor with the steel blade or into a blender. Blend until smooth. Cover and refrigerate for several hours before serving. Cut a slice off the top of the Hawaiian bread, and scoop bread out of the center of the loaf, leaving the shell with ½ inch of bread intact. Cube the scooped-out bread. Fill the cavity of the loaf with the chilled dip. Serve the bread cubes for dipping along with a platter of fresh vegetable sticks for dipping.

Pretty, easy, tasty, and certainly a change from "The Same Old Dip" routine. Hawaiian bread can be bought in most "deli" sections of the market.

Hot Olive Puffs

1 cup sharp Cheddar cheese, grated	½ teaspoon Worcestershire sauce
3 tablespoons margarine, softened	Dash of cayenne pepper
½ cup plain flour	Salt to taste
1 teaspoon paprika	35 medium stuffed green olives, very well drained

Preheat oven to 400°. In an electric mixer, cream the cheese and margarine. Blend in flour, paprika, Worcestershire sauce, cayenne pepper, and salt, if needed. Take a piece of dough, and roll into a ball; flatten the ball. Place a well-drained olive in the center of the flattened ball; then form the dough around the olive to cover completely. Arrange on an ungreased cookie sheet, and bake in the 400° oven for 12 minutes or until golden brown. Keep hot on a warming tray. Yield: 35.

For a variation, use walnuts, pecans, or almonds instead of olives. To help with measurements, figure 70 olives in a 10-ounce jar and double the recipe. A 13-ounce jar yields about 100 olives; triple the recipe. Olive Puffs may be made in advance and frozen on a cookie sheet; then remove to a Ziploc bag, and keep frozen until time to thaw and bake.

Stuffed Cherry Tomatoes

2 pounds bacon	½ cup mayonnaise
½ cup green onions, minced	24 cherry tomatoes, washed and dried

Dice raw bacon; then fry slowly until very crisp. Drain and cool on paper towels. In a bowl, combine cooled bacon, green onions, and mayonnaise; mix well. Remove any stems from the tomatoes. Place tomatoes, stem side down, on a cutting board, and slice a thin layer off the top. With a small scoop or spoon, scoop out most of the pulp. Invert tomato shells to drain for 30 minutes. Fill the shells with the bacon mixture. Refrigerate for several hours or overnight. Yield: 24 cherry tomatoes.

Confetti Cheesecake

1 cup sour cream
¼ cup green onion, finely chopped
3 tablespoons green olives with pimentos, finely chopped
¼ cup celery, finely chopped
2 tablespoons onion, finely chopped

1 teaspoon lemon juice
½ teaspoon Worcestershire sauce
Dash paprika
2 or 3 drops Tabasco sauce
⅔ cup (about 16) Ritz crackers, crushed very fine
Extra Ritz cracker crumbs to garnish

Combine all ingredients except cracker crumbs. Line a 2½ cup bowl with plastic wrap; then make layers of sour cream mixture and cracker crumbs. Begin with sour cream mixture and end with cracker crumbs. Cover and refrigerate overnight. Just before serving, turn out onto a serving plate and remove the plastic wrap. Sprinkle the extra Ritz crumbs on the top to garnish. Serve on crackers.

Artichoke Bites

2 (6-ounce) jars marinated artichoke hearts
2 medium onions, minced
1 large clove garlic, minced
4 eggs
¼ cup seasoned bread crumbs
½ teaspoon salt

⅛ teaspoon pepper
⅛ teaspoon crushed oregano
⅛ teaspoon Tabasco sauce
10 ounces sharp Cheddar cheese, grated
⅛ teaspoon garlic salt
2 tablespoons minced parsley

Preheat oven to 325°. Drain marinade from 1 jar of artichokes into a skillet. Drain the other jar of artichokes, and discard its marinade. Chop artichokes, and set aside. Cook the onion and garlic in the marinade until onion is soft. In a bowl, beat eggs until fluffy; then add bread crumbs, salt, pepper, oregano, and Tabasco sauce. Stir to mix, and add cheese, garlic salt, parsley, artichokes, and the onion mixture. Blend well, and pour into a greased 7×11-inch baking dish. Bake in the preheated 325° oven for 30 minutes. Allow to cool in the dish; then cut into 1-inch squares. Serve warm. Yield: 6 dozen.

Lasagna Crisps

1 **pound lasagna noodles**	**1-2 packages Good Seasons Italian Salad Dressing Mix, dry**

Cook noodles as directed on the package. Drain well, and spread onto waxed paper; then blot with paper to absorb extra moisture. With kitchen scissors, cut noodles crosswise into six 2-inch pieces. In an electric skillet, heat 1-1½ inches vegetable oil to 370°. Fry the cooked noodles until golden brown on both sides, about 5 minutes. Drain well on paper towels, do not stack. Pour the dry salad mix into a sturdy plastic bag and shake with the noodles for a light coat of seasonings. When noodles are completely cooled, store in a tightly covered container for as long as a week. Yield: 1 pound.

Hot Nuts

2	**tablespoons crushed red pepper (yes, tablespoons!)**	12	**ounce can Spanish peanuts**
3	**tablespoons olive oil**	12	**ounce can cocktail peanuts**
4	**small cloves garlic, crushed**	1	**teaspoon salt**
		1	**teaspoon chili powder**

In a skillet on medium high, heat red pepper in the oil for 1 minute, stirring constantly to prevent burning. Crush garlic, and add to oil. Then add both kinds of peanuts, and cook over medium heat for 5 minutes, while stirring. Remove from heat, and add salt and chili powder; toss well. Drain on paper towels, and cool completely. Store in the original peanut cans in the refrigerator.

Beverages

Champagne and Strawberry Punch

2 pints whole fresh
   strawberries
⅔ cup Grand Marnier
1 cup Cognac

2 fifths champagne, chilled
1 quart ginger ale, chilled
Block of ice

Thoroughly wash strawberries, leaving the hulls intact; drain. Place strawberries in a bowl with the Grand Marnier and Cognac ½ hour before serving time; refrigerate. At serving time, place strawberry mixture into punch bowl. Gently add champagne, ginger ale, and ice. Gently stir to mix.

Devil's Brew

1 fifth light rum
1 fifth sauterne
Ice rings or block ice

2 (28-ounce) bottles ginger ale
2 (28-ounce) bottles club soda

Chill all liquid ingredients. When chilled, mix rum and sauterne in a punch bowl. Add ice ring. Gently pour in the ginger ale and soda; mix to blend. Serves 17 (6-ounce) cups.

The mixture is well-named — it is smooth, tastes so good, and appears so innocent. Don't be fooled; it's very devilish!

Twenty-four Hour Cocktail

12 lemons	4 cups hot water
4 oranges	1 quart bourbon
2⅔ cups sugar	

In a large glass bowl, squeeze lemons and oranges; then cut up the rinds, and place in the bowl. Stir in the sugar and the hot water; mix very well. Pour in the bourbon; mix and cover. Allow the bourbon mixture to stand at room temperature for 24 hours. After 24 hours, strain and bottle the cocktail. Refrigerate until ready to serve.

This is a very powerful cocktail. If you prefer it a little less potent, add club soda, ginger ale, or both in portions suitable to your taste.

Rose Mary's Sangria

Make at least the day before serving.

1 fifth dry red wine	Orange slices
1 ounce Triple Sec	Lemon slices
1 cup brandy	Lime slices
½ cup lemon juice	1 pint fresh strawberries,
½ cup sugar	sliced
	1½ cups club soda

Mix wine, Triple Sec, brandy, lemon juice, and sugar. Add orange, lemon, and lime slices. Cover and refrigerate overnight. One hour before serving, sprinkle strawberries with extra brandy and add to Sangria. To serve, add club soda and stir.

Triple this recipe to use in a punch bowl with ice rings. Add any other fresh fruits that are available and appealing, such as peaches, mangoes, papayas, etc.

Mike's Moose Milk

½ gallon vanilla ice cream
1½ quarts milk
1   (16-ounce) bottle of creme de
    cacao

1   quart Half and Half
Pinch of nutmeg
1   (35-ounce) bottle of rum

Break ice cream into chunks and stir in all other ingredients. These measurements are all approximate. Juggle them around, according to taste, consistency desired, and alcoholic content desired. Serve immediately.

*Love the name! It comes, with the instructions, from our Canadian friends, Mike and Rose Mary. On the North Atlantic coast on a January evening, they've been known to use only a **scoop** of ice cream. My sentiments exactly.*

Sparkling Peach Punch

1   (29-ounce) can sliced
    peaches
1¼ cups Curacao or peach
    brandy

1   gallon Rhine wine
Block of ice
2   quarts ginger ale

Several hours before serving time, drain peaches, and place in a bowl with the Curacao; refrigerate. Just before serving, place peach and Curacao mixture into punch bowl. Gently add the wine, ice, and ginger ale. Stir gently to mix.

Have a few wooden skewers handy for the lucky guests at the end of the evening who get to eat the peaches. Ummm . . . delicious.

Spiked Watermelon

1 watermelon	⅓ cup sugar
1 cup orange juice	½ cup rum

Holding the melon lengthwise, cut off the top quarter in a scallop pattern, and remove all the watermelon meat. Remove seeds from enough meat to make 1 cup juice when pureed. In a bowl, add watermelon juice, orange juice, sugar, and rum. Stir until all the sugar has dissolved. Make melon balls of the remaining meat, removing as much seed as possible. Finally, return the melon balls to the watermelon shell, and pour the juice over them. Cover with plastic wrap, and refrigerate for several hours or overnight before serving. Serve with cocktail forks or long wooden skewers.

There will probably be a request or two for straws when all the melon balls are finished, to get the last drop of juice!

Brandy Alexander

½ cup brandy	1 quart vanilla ice cream
½ cup creme de cacao	Shaved chocolate, for garnish

Place all ingredients into a blender. Blend thoroughly. Pour into champagne glasses, and top with shaved chocolate.

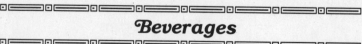
Mint Julep

½   tumbler crushed ice
1   tablespoon sugar

1   large bunch of freshly picked
    mint
Spirits

Crush the mint with the ice and sugar, add spirits to taste, then fill the glass with the rest of the mint and ice.

Have quoted this old recipe as it was originally written. The recipe was given to my great grandmother shortly after the turn of the century by a favorite cousin of hers from Richmond, Virginia. The "spirits" used would probably have been bourbon — try 2 ounces of good bourbon; and, of course, the "tumbler" must be sterling silver!

Piña Colada

7   ounces rum
8   ounces pineapple juice
4   ounces Coco Lopez Cream of
    Coconut

4   cups crushed ice
Fresh pineapple chunks for
  garnish

Place all ingredients except ice and garnish into a blender; blend. Add the crushed ice and blend until smooth. Pour into stemmed glasses and garnish with fresh pineapple chunks. Serves 4.

Kahlua

1   quart water
2½ cups sugar
4   tablespoons instant coffee

2½ cups vodka
1   tablespoon vanilla

In a saucepan, bring water, sugar, and coffee to a boil. Simmer very lightly for 3 hours. Add vodka and vanilla; stir. Refrigerate for at least a week before serving. Store in refrigerator. Yield: 1 quart plus.

Strip and Go Naked

1 tablespoon sugar syrup	Shaved ice
Juice of 1 lemon	Cold beer
2 ounces gin or vodka	

To make the syrup, heat 1 tablespoon sugar in a few drops of water until dissolved. Mix syrup, lemon juice, and gin or vodka; stir well. Pour into a tall glass; add shaved ice, and fill the remainder of the glass with beer. Stir.

Sounds horrible . . . tastes great . . . no comment on what it might do!

Egg Nog

6 eggs, separated and room temperature	6 tablespoons bourbon
8 tablespoons sugar, divided	½ pint whipping cream
	Nutmeg (optional)

In an electric mixer, beat egg yolks for 4 minutes; add 3 tablespoons of the sugar, and beat another 1 minute. Gradually beat in the bourbon until well blended and set yolks aside. Wash beater blades and chill in the freezer for a few minutes. Using another bowl that has been chilled, whip cream, and sweeten with 2 tablespoons of the sugar. Set cream aside. Wash beater blades. In a large bowl, beat egg whites until very stiff, but not dry. Add remaining 3 tablespoons sugar, and beat until well blended. Gently fold the yolk mixture into the egg whites; then fold in the whipped cream. Spoon into goblets or glasses, and serve immediately. Serve with a long silver spoon since the Egg Nog is thick and frothy. Sprinkle with nutmeg, if desired. Serves 6.

On a cold December evening, I like to remember my grandmother making Egg Nog. Her measurement of the bourbon was slightly inaccurate and certainly on the generous side. There were never any complaints. If you should need more than 6 servings, use 1 egg, 1 tablespoon sugar, and 1 "generous" tablespoon bourbon per serving. Adjust the sweetened whipped cream accordingly.

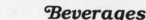

Dear's Tea — A Delightfully Different Iced Tea

8 cups boiling water
1 cup sugar
1 family size teabag
1 small teabag

Juice of ½ lemon
4 tablespoons unsweetened grape juice

Add boiling water to a pitcher. Stir in the sugar until completely dissolved. Add both teabags to the boiling water, and tie the teabag strings to the handle of the pitcher for easy removal later. Cover the pitcher, and allow to steep overnight or until completely cooled. Remove teabags. Stir in the lemon juice and grape juice. Refrigerate, covered, until chilled. Yield: 2 quarts.

Back in the good "old" days before air conditioning, I loved to visit my grandmother and have her "Dear's Tea" to cool off. Now in the good "new" days, I still love to visit the old home where my aunt always offers me "Dear's Tea." Simple pleasures, long remembered.

Frothy Orange Slush

1 (6-ounce) can frozen orange juice concentrate, undiluted
1 cup water
¼ cup sugar

⅓ cup milk
1 teaspoon vanilla
12 ice cubes

Mix all ingredients in a blender until ice cubes make a slush. Pour into glasses, and drink immediately. Store unused portion in the freezer.

Soups, Salads, and Sandwiches

Joan's Mobile Seafood Gumbo

Make one day before serving.

5 tablespoons bacon drippings
6 tablespoons plain flour
2 large onions, chopped fine
2 cups celery, chopped fine
1 large green pepper, chopped fine
4 cloves garlic, crushed
2 tablespoons parsley flakes
4 whole bay leaves
1 (28-ounce) can tomatoes, chopped
1 (15-ounce) can tomato sauce
3 teaspoons salt
1 teaspoon pepper
2 quarts water
3 cups chopped fresh okra or 2 (10-ounce) packages frozen okra, cut
2 pounds raw shrimp, peeled
8 to 12 cleaned crab backs or 1 pound crabmeat
3 tablespoons Worcestershire sauce
2 or more drops Tabasco sauce
2 tablespoons filé
Hot rice

Using an iron skillet, make the roux by melting the bacon drippings over moderate heat; then add flour, 1 tablespoon at a time, keeping the roux smooth. Roux must be stirred constantly to get a very dark color, but not burn. If it should burn, throw out, and begin again. Take your time to get a dark caramel color. Lower heat, if necessary, and keep stirring. When roux is finished, remove from heat, and set aside. In a large, heavy soup pot, add onions, celery, green pepper, garlic, parsley, bay leaves, chopped tomatoes, tomato sauce, salt, pepper, and water; stir. Bring to a boil, and reduce heat to simmer. Cook, uncovered, for 2 hours. After the 2 hours, scoop up a cup of liquid, and slowly add to the roux, keeping roux smooth. Add another cup of the hot liquid to the roux until the roux is the consistency of the gumbo. Add liquified roux to the soup pot, and stir well. Add okra, and continue to cook and stir for ½ hour. Then add shrimp, crab backs or crabmeat, Worcestershire sauce, Tabasco sauce, and filé. Continue cooking for another ½ to 1 hour; then test for salt. Stir frequently at this stage of cooking. Let Gumbo cool, and refrigerate overnight. When ready to serve, reheat very slowly; stir often, being careful not to let the Gumbo stick. Remove bay leaves and discard. Serve over hot rice in soup bowls. Gumbo freezes very well. Serves 8 to 10.

Nothing else is needed with this Gumbo, but fresh, hot French bread, plenty of time to enjoy it, and good company to enjoy it with.

Crab Bisque

6 tablespoons margarine, divided
4 tablespoons green pepper, minced
4 tablespoons onion, minced
1 green onion with top, minced
2 tablespoons parsley, minced
1½ cups sliced fresh mushrooms
2 tablespoons plain flour

1 cup milk
1 teaspoon salt
⅛ teaspoon pepper
1 drop Tabasco sauce
1½ cups Half and Half
1½ cups crabmeat
1 tablespoon dry sherry (optional)

In a skillet, heat 4 tablespoons of the margarine; then add green pepper, onion, green onion, parsley, and mushrooms. Sauté until soft, about 5 minutes. In a saucepan, melt remaining 2 tablespoons margarine; then stir in flour until smooth. Gradually add milk, stirring and heating over medium heat until thickened and smooth. Stir in salt, pepper, Tabasco sauce, sautéed vegetables, and Half and Half. Bring to a boil, stirring; then reduce heat to simmer, and add crabmeat. Simmer uncovered for 5 minutes. When ready to serve, stir in the sherry. Serves 4.

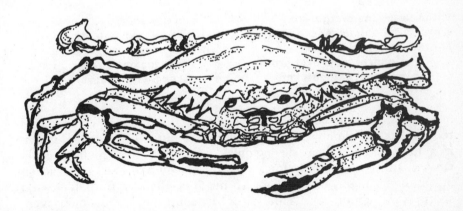

Marvelous Hot Vichyssoise

6 medium Idaho potatoes, cooked in salted water, peeled, and cubed	6 ounces cream cheese, softened
6 green onions, sliced	Salt
2 medium onions, chopped	2 drops Tabasco sauce
1½ quarts chicken broth or stock	Chopped chives
	Paprika

In a Dutch oven, add cooked potatoes, green onion, chopped onions, and chicken broth. Bring to a boil; then reduce heat to simmer, and cook 45 minutes. Place the potato mixture in a food processor with the steel blade or in a blender; then add the cream cheese, cut in chunks, and puree until very smooth. Add salt to taste and Tabasco sauce. Return soup to Dutch oven to reheat. Serve hot, topped with chives and paprika. Serves 8 or more.

I know, I know; obviously I flunked French! Vichyssoise is supposed to be served cold. Regardless, I like it hot. Give it a try.

Jay's French Onion Soup

6 tablespoons margarine	¼ cup dry sherry
4 to 5 large onions, sliced thin	Salt and pepper to taste
1 tablespoon plain flour	Grated Parmesan cheese
2 (10½-ounce) cans beef broth	6 slices toasted French bread
1 (10½-ounce) can chicken broth	6 slices Swiss cheese

In a skillet, melt margarine, and add onions. Bring to a boil, cover, and reduce heat to simmer. Cook slowly for about 20 minutes. Remove from heat, and add flour, stirring quickly. Return to medium heat, cooking and stirring constantly for 1 minute. Slowly add beef and chicken broth; then simmer, covered, for 15 minutes. Remove from heat. Add sherry and pepper; check for salt. Pour soup into 6 individual ovenproof tureens; sprinkle with Parmesan cheese, float the toast, and cover toast with Swiss cheese slice. Place under oven broiler until cheese melts. Serves 6.

Mushroom and Barley Soup

1 pound fresh mushrooms, rinsed and drained
6 tablespoons margarine, divided
1 cup onion, minced
1 clove garlic, minced
2 (10¾-ounce) cans condensed beef broth
5 soup cans of water
3 tablespoons catsup

¾ teaspoon salt
⅛ teaspoon pepper
1 bay leaf
½ cup uncooked barley
¼ cup parsley, chopped
1½ cups celery, sliced including the chopped leaves
1½ cups carrots, sliced round
4 tablespoons dry sherry
Sour cream, if desired

Chop ½ of the mushrooms, and slice ½ of the mushrooms. In a large saucepan, melt 4 tablespoons margarine, and add chopped mushrooms, onions, and garlic; sauté for 5 minutes. Stir in broth, water, catsup, salt, pepper, and bay leaf. Heat to boiling; then stir in barley, and reduce heat. Cover and simmer for 1 hour. Add parsley, celery, and carrots; cook, covered, for 30 minutes longer or until barley and vegetables are tender. In a medium skillet, melt remaining 2 tablespoons margarine, and sauté the sliced mushrooms for 5 minutes. Add these mushrooms along with the sherry to the soup, and stir. Remove bay leaf and discard. Serve in large soup bowls with a dollop of sour cream, if desired. Serves 8.

The soup is hearty, delicious, and a little different. Great both as a soup course served in a tureen, or as a light supper served with fresh, hot French bread by the fire on a cold night.

Soup for One

1 medium onion, chopped
1 medium potato, peeled and sliced

1 cup rich chicken broth
1 cup milk
Salt and pepper to taste

Boil the onion and potato in a small amount of salted water until very tender. Drain onion and potato, and press through a sieve or put in a blender for a couple of seconds. Add the blended potato and onion to the chicken broth; stir in the milk. Heat until thoroughly hot; add salt and pepper to taste. Yield: 2 cups.

Beefsteak Soup

1 pound round steak, chopped fine
1 cup margarine, divided
1 cup plain flour
1½ tablespoons MSG
Salt and pepper to taste
1 large onion, chopped fine
1 large carrot, chopped fine
3 ribs celery, chopped fine

1 #2½ can tomatoes, chopped fine
1 tablespoon Worcestershire sauce
4 (10½-ounce) cans consommé
54 ounces water
6 teaspoons granulated beef bouillon
1½ cups Half and Half

Stir-fry beef in ½ the margarine until browned. Add flour, MSG, salt, and pepper to taste. In another skillet, sauté onion, carrot, celery, and tomatoes in the remaining margarine until tender. Add vegetable mixture to the beef mixture; stir well. Add Worcestershire sauce, consommé, water, and beef bouillon. Stir to dissolve bouillon. Bring to a boil; reduce heat, and simmer for 1 hour. Add Half and Half to the soup before serving; heat, but do not boil. Yield: about 1 gallon.

Emerald Soup

Use the microwave to make this soup.

1 (15-ounce) can spinach, drained and pureed
3 slices bacon, cooked and crumbled
2 tablespoons parsley, chopped
½ teaspoon seasoned salt
1 (10½-ounce) can consommé

¼ cup onion, minced
1 small clove garlic, minced
½ teaspoon basil
⅛ teaspoon pepper
1 pint Half and Half
Parmesan cheese, grated
Paprika
Seasoned croutons

Mix spinach, crumbled bacon, parsley, seasoned salt, consommé, onion, garlic, basil, and pepper in a glass bowl; cover and cook on full power in the microwave for 14 minutes. Let soup completely cool; then add Half and Half. Stir and cook again on full power for about 2 minutes or until heated. Serve topped with lots of Parmesan cheese and some paprika. Add seasoned croutons, if desired. Serves 2 to 4.

South of the Border Soup

2   (15-ounce) cans pinto beans
½   pound lean ham, diced
3   slices bacon, cooked crisp
    and crumbled
1   tablespoon bacon drippings

½   teaspoon ground cumin
1   medium onion, minced
1   cup water
1   medium clove garlic, minced

Combine all ingredients in a heavy pot. Bring to a boil; then reduce the heat to simmer. Cook for 30 to 45 minutes, uncovered. Add a small amount of extra water, if needed. Serves 4.

This soup is very authentic when served with soft, steamed tortillas "slathered" in butter and rolled. Muy bueno!

Natty's Cuban Black Bean Soup

4   tablespoons vegetable oil
2   medium onions, chopped
2   medium green peppers,
    chopped
3   large cloves garlic, minced
3   cups water
4   teaspoons dry beef bouillon

2   teaspoons ground cumin
2   teaspoons crushed oregano
    leaves
2   tablespoons wine vinegar
6   cups cooked black beans,
    drained

In a Dutch oven, heat oil over medium heat; then add onion, green pepper, and garlic. Cook until limp; add water, bouillon, cumin, oregano, vinegar, and beans. Cover, and reduce heat to simmer; cook 30 minutes. Serve in soup bowls over hot rice with minced onion on top.

A great soup all by itself. If you're feeling a little Latin, make a dinner of it, with Fried Plantains (see Vegetables) and A Little Cuban Cube Steak (see Beef Entrées).

Woody's Camp Stew

Make at least 1 day before serving.

5   chicken fryers, 2½ to 3 pounds each

12 to 15 pork chops

3   pounds onions, chopped

64   ounces catsup

16   ounces prepared mustard

1   teaspoon cayenne pepper

5   pounds Irish potatoes, peeled and diced fine

4   (16-ounce) cans cream-style corn

1   (10-ounce) bottle Durkee Famous Sauce

1   (10-ounce) bottle Worcestershire sauce

Boil fryers in salted water in a heavy pot large enough to completely cover the fryers with the water. Cook until very tender, and remove from the bones. Discard skin and bones. Save the chicken stock for later use. Smoke pork chops on a covered grill, slowly to keep moist, until barely tender; remove from grill. Cool chops and take meat from the bones; discard bones and dice pork meat. In a 5-gallon heavy pot, add chicken meat, pork meat, and all the other ingredients; then fill the pot to about ¾ full with the reserved chicken stock. Keep any remaining stock for thinning stew later, if it is needed. Bring the stew to a boil; then reduce heat to a bare simmer. The stew will stick to the pot very easily, so it needs to be stirred very, very often (take turns—"While you're up, stir the Stew!"). It needs to be stirred from the bottom since the heavy ingredients sink. Cook on very low heat for about 8 hours or until the potatoes are soft and crumbling. Cool and refrigerate overnight. When ready to serve, reheat very slowly at a very low heat, stirring almost constantly.

This is a project! It is easiest with 2 or more people making the stew in 2 stages. One day to chop, cut, and get meats ready, and the next day to cook. Don't forget cooling time before refrigerating and space in the refrigerator. Now, for the rewards, one bowlful should tell it all. The stew serves a crowd and even more of a crowd if barbecued meat is being served with it. Freezes very well. Perfect for outdoor holidays with everyone in a picnic mood, except poor Woody with "stirrer's elbow."

Albert Gresham's Camp Stew

This recipe is made every Fourth of July and Labor Day in old iron washpots over a fire. Until just a couple of years before his 98th birthday, "Mr. Albert," or "Pop," supervised the all night making of this stew. So if you have a washpot that is clean, a sturdy boat paddle for stirring, all day to cut ingredients, and all night to cook, have a go at it.

8 pounds pork	Salt, pepper, and cayenne
2 (5-pound) hens, stewed, bones removed, and cutup	pepper to taste
12 pounds potatoes, cubed	6 pounds onions, chopped
1 gallon cream-style corn	1 gallon tomato puree
1 pint Worcestershire sauce	1 pint prepared mustard
2 whole stalks celery, chopped	2 quarts water

Cook pork and hens until tender; then cook vegetables in the stock. Mix all together, and cook some more . . . This makes about 50 servings. If served with barbecued meat, 1 gallon will serve about 16. If served by itself, 1 gallon will serve about 10.

I must confess I haven't tested this recipe 'cause my washpot is full of clothes, and it ain't Monday yet.

Gazpacho

2 (10½-ounce) cans consommé	1 (46-ounce) can V-8 Juice
1 small clove garlic, crushed	1 small onion, minced
1 large fresh tomato, peeled and chopped	1 medium cucumber, peeled and minced
3 tablespoons olive oil	1 tablespoon lime juice
½ teaspoon sugar	Salt to taste
Tabasco sauce to taste	Pepper to taste

Combine all ingredients, and mix well. Cover and refrigerate overnight. Remove garlic. Serve with croutons.

Great served at a summer brunch or as the soup course for a luncheon.

Colonial Chicken and Corn Soup

4 ounces chicken breast, cooked and minced	4 cups chicken stock
	Salt to taste
1 (16-ounce) can cream-style corn	4 tablespoons cornstarch
	1 egg white
1 tablespoon vegetable oil	4 slices bacon, cooked and crumbled
1 tablespoon cooking sherry	

Combine minced chicken and creamed corn; set aside. In a large saucepan, heat oil and sherry to just below boiling; immediately add chicken stock, and stir to mix. Bring mixture to a boil, and add chicken and corn mixture. Add salt to taste. Mix cornstarch with a few drops of cold water until smooth; then stir into the soup. Continue heating and stirring soup until thickened. Beat egg white, by hand, until slightly frothy. Very slowly stir the egg white into the gently boiling soup. At serving time pour soup into a tureen and sprinkle with the crumbled bacon.

Sal's Cold Squash Soup

1 pound yellow squash, cubed
1 medium onion, chopped very fine
1 (14½-ounce) can chicken broth
1 tablespoon margarine
2 teaspoons dry chicken bouillon

1 cup boiling water
1 tablespoon Worcestershire sauce
½ teaspoon oregano
Salt and pepper to taste
8 ounces sour cream

Cook squash and onion in chicken broth for about 15 minutes or until tender. Remove from heat, and add margarine and the chicken bouillon dissolved in the boiling water. Let cool; then stir in Worcestershire, oregano, and any additional salt and pepper required. Pour into food processor with steel blade or blender; blend until smooth. Pour into a refrigerator container, and stir in the sour cream. Mix well and refrigerate. Serves 4 to 6.

Salads

West Indies Salad

For best results, make no substitutions and follow directions exactly.

1 pound fresh lump crabmeat
4 ounces Wesson oil
4 ounces ice water
3 ounces cider vinegar

1 medium onion, chopped very fine
Salt and pepper to taste

Lightly toss all ingredients until well mixed, taking care not to break the crabmeat lumps. Cover tightly, and marinate overnight. Stir occasionally to marinate evenly. Drain each serving, and serve cold. Keep refrigerated. Serves 4-6.

This is unsurpassable crab. Keeping "hands-off" for 24 hours during the marinating time will be the biggest problem.

Shrimp Salad

1 pound fresh shrimp, cooked and peeled	¾ cup mayonnaise
1 teaspoon green pepper, minced	2 tablespoons onion, minced
	1 tablespoon celery, minced
¼ teaspoon salt	2 teaspoons lemon juice
Dash pepper	1 drop Tabasco sauce
	Paprika

Chop shrimp, and mix with all other ingredients. Refrigerate for several hours or overnight. Serve cold on a lettuce cup or stuffed into a tomato. Garnish with a little paprika. Serves 2 to 3.

Crab Louis

Shredded lettuce	1 drop Tabasco sauce
Fresh salad greens	2 tablespoons lemon juice
2 pounds cold crabmeat	8 hard-boiled eggs
2 cups mayonnaise	18 cherry tomatoes
1 cup chili sauce	12 large black olives or green
2 cloves garlic, minced	stuffed olives

Arrange shredded lettuce over a bed of the salad greens on 6 individual large, main course salad plates. Pile the crabmeat on top of the shredded lettuce. In a bowl, blend mayonnaise, chili sauce, garlic, Tabasco, and lemon juice; beat well. Split in half all 8 peeled hard-boiled eggs. Scoop out the yolks of 2 whole eggs, and mash very fine. Blend the mashed yolks into the dressing, and spoon dressing over the crabmeat. Garnish each plate with 1 egg quartered, 3 cherry tomatoes, 2 olives, and finish with the remaining egg white chipped very fine and sprinkled over the dressing. Refrigerate until serving time. Serves 6.

A treat to the eye as well as the palate!

Crab Salad Pyramids

Sauce: prepare 1 day before serving.

1   cup mayonnaise
1   teaspoon vinegar
1   teaspoon Worcestershire
    sauce

3   teaspoons anchovy paste
1   cup chili sauce
1 to 3 drops Tabasco sauce
1   tablespoon onion, grated

Base:

4 to 6 Holland rusks
3   ounces cream cheese,
    softened
Mayonnaise
Lettuce
2   large tomatoes, peeled and
    sliced

1   large avocado, peeled and
    sliced
1 or 2 hard-boiled eggs, peeled
    and sliced
1   pound lump crabmeat

To prepare sauce, mix all the sauce ingredients, and chill in the refrigerator overnight. To prepare the base, spread the Holland rusk with the cream cheese that has been softened to spreading consistency with mayonnaise. Place the rusk on a large bed of lettuce, and top with tomato slice, avocado slices, and egg slices. Add cold crabmeat, divided evenly, and cover with the sauce. Serves 4 to 6.

Great Chicken Salad

1   (3-pound) fryer
2   hard-boiled eggs
3 or 4 large ribs celery, chopped

1   whole dill pickle, chopped
¾ to 1 cup mayonnaise

Boil the fryer in salted water until very tender. Drain, cool, and remove meat from the bone. Cut the chicken meat in medium size pieces. Mash hard-boiled eggs if still hot, or chop fine if cold. Combine chicken, celery, pickle, and eggs; toss to mix. Stir in the mayonnaise to taste and consistency desired. Cover and refrigerate, allowing flavors to blend for several hours. Serve as a salad, sandwich spread, or on toast rounds as a canapé.

Oriental Chicken Salad

The very thin noodles used in this recipe are found in an Oriental food market. They are translucent and are called rice vermicelli. When fried, they expand very quickly and some may even "jump" out of the skillet. The noodles can be cooked 1 day in advance, if stored in an airtight container. Prepare the recipe 4 to 6 hours before serving.

Vegetable oil for frying
1   ounce rice vermicelli noodles
¾   cup vegetable oil
6   tablespoons vinegar
½   teaspoon sugar
2   teaspoons soy sauce
½   teaspoon salt
½   teaspoon ground ginger
⅛   teaspoon pepper

3   cups cubed, cooked chicken
1   head iceberg lettuce, very thinly shredded
4   green onions, sliced diagonally
4   teaspoons sesame seeds, toasted
½   cup sliced almonds, toasted

Heat 2 inches of oil in a 10-inch skillet or a wok to 375°. Drop a small handful of noodles (remember the expansion) into the oil. Cook only until noodles puff and turn opaque. Turn the entire mass of noodles over to cook on reverse side. When noodles stop crackling, remove with a slotted spoon. Drain on paper towels. Cook remaining noodles. About 4 to 6 hours before serving time, combine vegetable oil, vinegar, sugar, soy, salt, ginger, and pepper. Place in a jar with a tight-fitting lid, and shake vigorously. When dressing is well-mixed, pour enough dressing over the chicken to marinate. Reserve remaining dressing and refrigerate. Toss chicken to thoroughly coat with the dressing, and refrigerate, covered for 4 to 6 hours. At serving time, use a large salad bowl to combine lettuce, marinated chicken, onions, noodles, sesame seeds, and almonds. Add reserved dressing, and toss well. Served 4 to 6.

Chicken Salad Veronique

Prepare and refrigerate salad overnight before serving.

2 cups cooked chicken, cubed	¼ cup sour cream
¾ cup celery, sliced very thin	1 cup green, seedless grapes, halved
¼ cup slivered almonds, toasted	2 teaspoons soy sauce
1 teaspoon salt	½ cup mayonnaise

Mix all ingredients until well blended. More soy sauce can be added, if desired. Refrigerate in a covered glass bowl overnight before serving. Serves 4 to 6.

Have you ever been served chicken salad and seriously wondered if it weren't really wet cardboard? There's no similarity here! Serve the salad many ways—stuffed in an avocado, a tomato, a cantaloupe, individual noodle birdnest basket, or flour tortilla shell, etc.

Crunchy Tuna Salad

1 (6½-ounce) can water-packed tuna, drained	1 very small onion, minced
1 stalk celery, minced	1 small apple, peeled and chopped
8 to 10 pecans, chopped	Mayonnaise
Salt to taste	

Mix all ingredients and adjust mayonnaise to desired consistency. Refrigerate.

All of the goodies that "go crunch" make this an interesting, different Tuna Salad with a delightful flavor.

Tom's Terrific Slaw

There's a secret to this recipe—how the cabbage is shredded! Select a hard, non-leafy cabbage, and cut it into quarters. To get long, thin shreds of cabbage, finely shred the quartered cabbage on the longest surface with a steel-blade vegetable slicer, or use a sharp knife and shred by hand. The slaw does not taste the same if it is chopped or coarse. Truly, the extra effort is worth the taste.

4 cups thinly shredded cabbage, packed firmly in the cup	**⅛** teaspoon crushed red pepper (can be omitted)
½ teaspoon salt	**½** teaspoon celery seed (do not omit)
½ teaspoon garlic salt	**2 to 2½** tablespoons Wesson oil
¼ teaspoon black pepper	**1** tablespoon white vinegar

Place the shredded cabbage in a large bowl with room to toss. Sprinkle salt, garlic salt, black pepper, red pepper, and celery seed evenly on top of cabbage; then pour oil over the spices. Toss well to distribute spices and oil. Finally, add vinegar, and toss again. If slaw is too tart for your taste, add a pinch of sugar to "tone-down" the vinegar. Cover and refrigerate. Serves 4.

My father concocted this slaw recipe years ago. It is often requested with seldom any left. If any remains, some people prefer it a day old after it has marinated. The recipe can be doubled or tripled. It appears to be a great mound of cabbage when you begin. Then after adding the ingredients, it suddenly drops to half its volume! Do not despair; it's just packed and will serve more than you realize.

Layered Spinach Salad

Make one day in advance of serving and refrigerate.

1   pint mayonnaise
8   ounces sour cream
1   teaspoon lemon juice
1   cup Swiss cheese
1   large bag fresh spinach, washed, dried, chilled, and torn in pieces
½   pound bacon, fried crisp and crumbled

1   (10-ounce) package frozen green peas
½   head lettuce, washed, dried, chilled, and torn in pieces
3   hard boiled eggs, peeled and chopped
½   medium onion, chopped
¼   teaspoon sugar
Salt and pepper to taste

Combine mayonnaise, sour cream, lemon juice, and Swiss cheese; mix well. Make layers in a casserole or glass bowl beginning with spinach. Add bacon, uncooked frozen green peas, lettuce, chopped eggs, and chopped onion. Sprinkle salad with sugar, salt, and pepper. Top with the dressing. If bowl is narrow at the top, all the dressing may not be needed. Cover salad and refrigerate overnight. Serves 12 to 15.

Fresh Broccoli Salad

Prepare salad 1 day before serving.

2   bunches broccoli, cut into flowerets
1   small purple onion, sliced in rings
1   (4-ounce) can sliced mushrooms

1   (8-ounce) bottle Creamy Italian Dressing
1   (4-ounce) jar chopped pimentos
1   pound bacon, fried and crumbled

Mix all ingredients, except the bacon, and place in a crystal bowl; cover, and marinate in the refrigerator overnight. Before serving, sprinkle the top of the salad with the crumbled bacon. Serves 6.

Mushroom and Onion Salad

Prepare at least 4 hours before serving.

1   pound fresh small
    mushrooms, washed and
    sliced in half
1   large purple onion, sliced in
    thin rings
1   clove garlic, crushed

⅔   cup vinegar
¼   cup water
1½ teaspoons salt
Dash of pepper
2   tablespoons vegetable oil

Mix all ingredients in a glass bowl. Cover tightly and refrigerate. Drain
and remove garlic before serving. Serves 6 to 8.

*Very, very simple, yet always a highly requested recipe. This can also
serve as an appetizer. Any leftovers improve in flavor for at least 2 days.*

Turkish Salad

2   large tomatoes
½   large mild onion, chopped
2   medium cucumbers, peeled
    and chopped
½   cup fresh parsley, chopped

½   green pepper or a hot
    pepper, chopped
1   tablespoon olive oil
1½ lemons
Salt and pepper to taste

Chop tomatoes over a bowl to prevent any loss of juice; then add all
other chopped vegetables. Add oil and toss; then add the juice of the
lemons, and toss again. Salt and pepper to taste. Can be prepared
ahead of time and refrigerated. Serves 4.

*This salad is also wonderful as an appetizer served with tortilla rounds.
Very colorful.*

Garden Fresh Cucumbers

3	medium cucumbers	1	teaspoon sugar
¼	cup vinegar	⅛	teaspoon pepper
1	teaspoon celery seed	¼	cup onion, chopped
¾	teaspoon salt	2	tablespoons parsley, chopped
¼	teaspoon MSG, do not omit		
1	tablespoon lemon juice		

Wash cucumbers, and score the unpeeled sides by drawing a fork's tines down the length of the cucumber. Repeat process around the cucumber. Slice cucumbers in thin rounds. Mix all other ingredients; then add cucumber slices. Refrigerate, covered, for 6 hours or overnight before serving. Do not add more liquid since the cucumbers will lose water and increase the liquid. Stir occasionally. Drain to serve. Serves 4 to 6.

Butter Bean Salad

Marinate overnight.

1	(24-ounce) bag small butter beans or lima beans	½	cup vegetable oil
2	small to medium mild onions, sliced in thin rings	½	cup vinegar
		1	teaspoon salt
½	cup fresh parsley, chopped	¼	teaspoon pepper
			Pinch of sugar

Cook butter beans as directed on the package; drain. Place drained beans in a glass bowl; add onions and parsley. In a jar with a tight fitting cap, combine oil, vinegar, salt, pepper, and sugar. Shake until well-mixed; then pour over the butter bean mixture. Toss gently to mix all ingredients. Cover and refrigerate overnight. Drain before serving. Serves 6.

Jay's Elegant Potato Salad

6 large Idaho potatoes	½ cup celery, chopped fine
3-4 hard boiled eggs, peeled and chopped fine	1-2 tablespoons capers
White pepper to taste	1-2 tablespoons stuffed green olives, chopped (optional)
Salt to taste	4 ounces sour cream
1½ tablespoons tarragon or champagne white vinegar	4 ounces mayonnaise
3 green onions with tops, chopped	¼ cup buttermilk
	Parsley for garnish

Boil the unpeeled potatoes in salted water until tender. Drain, and allow potatoes to cool enough to handle; then peel, and cut into cubes. Add all other ingredients to the potato cubes except the parsley. Mix all ingredients thoroughly. Cover and refrigerate. Allow potato salad to chill for at least 4 hours; overnight is better. Garnish with parsley before serving. Serves 8 to 12.

Cranberry Pecan Salad

1 envelope unflavored gelatin	1 (16-ounce) can cranberry sauce
1 (3-ounce) package raspberry gelatin	1 (8¾-ounce) can crushed pineapple, drained
1 cup boiling water	¾ cup pecans, chopped

In an electric mixer bowl, completely dissolve both gelatins in the boiling water. Add cranberry sauce, and beat until gelatin mixture and cranberry sauce are well-blended. By hand, stir in the drained pineapple and pecans. Pour into a ring mold, and refrigerate until firmly set. Serves 6 to 8.

Traditionally served with Christmas dinner at our house. Top the salad with homemade mayonnaise, and it's wonderful with turkey and dressing. What makes it even better, my husband's aunt makes the salad, and his mother makes the mayonnaise. I graciously provide the salad plate and salad fork!

Tomato and Olive Aspic

4 cups V-8 juice, divided
⅓ cup onion, chopped
¼ cup celery leaves, chopped
2 tablespoons brown sugar
1 teaspoon salt
2 small bay leaves

4 whole cloves
3 envelopes unflavored gelatin
3 tablespoons lemon juice
1 cup celery, minced
½ cup stuffed green olives, chopped

In a saucepan, combine 2 cups of the V-8 juice with onion, celery leaves, brown sugar, salt, bay leaves, and cloves. Bring to a boil; then reduce heat, and simmer, uncovered, for 5 minutes. Strain the mixture into a bowl. Soften unflavored gelatin in 1 cup of the V-8 juice. When softened, add gelatin mixture to the hot liquid in the bowl, and stir to completely dissolve. Add remaining 1 cup V-8 juice and lemon juice. Stir well to blend. Refrigerate until partially set. Stir in celery and olives. Pour into a ring mold or flat casserole. Refrigerate until very firm. Serve topped with mayonnaise. Serves 6 to 8.

Sand Pail Salad

Great for picnics or for parties for children. Have a new, brightly colored plastic sand pail with the shovel to serve the salad.

1 (8-ounce) carton whipped topping
1 (16-ounce) can fruit cocktail, drained
1 (15½-ounce) can crushed pineapple, drained
1 teaspoon lemon juice

1 cup miniature marshmallows
Fresh fruit in season to fill the pail (sliced bananas, sliced apples, sliced peaches, grapes, melon, strawberries, etc.)
Chocolate wafers, crushed

Combine all ingredients except the chocolate wafers. Mix well, and fill the pail. Top with crushed chocolate wafers for the "dirt." Refrigerate salad to thoroughly chill before serving.

Summer Fruit Cup

1 large cantaloupe
1 (20-ounce) can pineapple
 chunks, drained
1 (11-ounce) can mandarin
 oranges, undrained

4 fresh, ripe peaches, peeled
 and sliced
½ cup sugar
Juice of 2 lemons

Peel cantaloupe and cut into chunks. Combine with remaining ingredients. Chill for several hours. The fruit will keep, when refrigerated, for about 4 days. Serves 6.

French Dressing

1 cup vegetable oil
4 tablespoons vinegar
1½ to 2 teaspoons salt
1 teaspoon paprika

4 tablespoons lemon juice
½ teaspoon dry mustard
½ teaspoon garlic powder
Dash cayenne pepper

Place all ingredients into a covered jar, and shake vigorously. Refrigerate for several hours before serving.

Roquefort Dressing

1 cup olive oil
½ cup vinegar
4 ounces Roquefort cheese,
 mashed
1 tablespoon lemon juice

1 teaspoon paprika
2 drops Worcestershire sauce
1 tablespoon onion, grated
Dash cayenne pepper
½ teaspoon salt

In a jar, add oil and vinegar and mix; then add all other ingredients. Mix very well. Cap jar tightly and refrigerate. Shake well before serving. The dressing's flavor improves with time. Yield: 2 cups.

Myra's Fruit Salad Dressing

⅓ cup sugar
3 tablespoons honey
1 teaspoon salt
1 teaspoon dry mustard

1 teaspoon celery seed
1 teaspoon paprika
1 cup vegetable oil
¼ cup vinegar

In an electric mixer, combine sugar with honey, salt, dry mustard, celery seed, and paprika. On medium speed, alternately add oil and vinegar, pouring in a slow stream. Pour dressing over a selection of melons, grapefruit and avocado salad, or other fruit salad. Refrigerate to store. Yield: 1⅔ cups.

Sandwiches

Oyster Loaf

Individual French loaves, split
Margarine
Fried oysters (see Seafood)

Quick, Great Cocktail Sauce (see Sauces)
Dill pickle slices

Split the French loaves, and spread both surfaces with margarine. Heat the loaves until bread is hot and margarine is melted. Fill the loaves with hot, crisp fried oysters. Cover tops of oysters with cocktail sauce and several pickle slices. Serve hot.

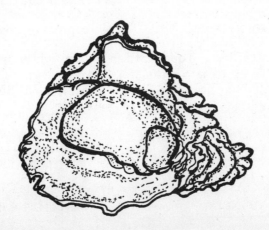

Creole Weiners

8 slices bacon, cut in ½-inch squares	¾ teaspoon salt
	⅛ teaspoon pepper
2½ cups tomatoes, chopped	1 pound weiners

In a skillet, cook bacon until half done. Drain most of the fat off, and continue cooking until golden brown. Stir in tomatoes, salt, and pepper. Cut weiners into 5 chunks each, and add to the skillet; stir and cover. Simmer gently for 45 minutes; then remove cover, and boil hard 5-10 minutes to reduce the liquid. Serve hot over rice or in buns. Serves 4.

Egg-Olive Sandwich Filling

4 eggs, hard boiled and chilled	¼ cup stuffed green olives, chopped
1½ tablespoons mayonnaise	Olive juice

Peel eggs, and chop. Add mayonnaise and chopped olives. Pour enough olive juice into mixture to make mixture spreadable as a sandwich filling. Refrigerate. Yield: 2-3 sandwiches.

Absolutely Scrumptious Crab-Wich

1 English muffin, half	Salt and pepper to taste
1 tablespoon mayonnaise	¼ cup crabmeat
1 slice tomato, peeled	¼ cup Colby cheese, grated

Preheat oven to 350°. Toast English muffin lightly and spread with mayonnaise. Place tomato on muffin, and salt; then mound crabmeat, and salt and pepper. Top with Colby cheese. Bake at 350° for about 5 minutes or until the cheese is melted. Serves 1.

Entrées

Standing Ribs of Beef

6-8 pound standing rib roast,
U.S. Choice

Trim excess fat off roast, leaving some fat on for flavor and juice. Position roast with the fat side up on a shallow baking pan. Do not salt, do not cover, and do not add any water to the pan — just cook it au natural. Cooking times listed below are for a roast just out of refrigerator, baked at 325°.

6 pounds: rare, 2¼ hours
　　　　　medium, 2½ hours
　　　　　well done, 3¼ hours

8 pounds: rare, 3 hours
　　　　　medium, 3½ hours
　　　　　well done, 4½ hours

Immediately after removing from the oven, salt and pepper the roast generously. The hot beef will draw in the flavors. Allow the serving time for dinner to accommodate a rest period of 15 to 25 minutes for the roast after removing from the oven. It will carve more easily. Heat the drippings to serve over the beef. Six pounds serves 12; eight pounds serves 14.

Save leftover ribs to prepare Deviled Rib Bones.

Deviled Rib Bones

Leftover standing rib bones　　**Melted margarine**
White vinegar　　　　　　　　**Italian bread crumbs**

Sprinkle vinegar on the rib bones, then dip into the melted margarine and roll to coat well in bread crumbs. Broil coated bones on all sides until browned.

*I do believe these are better than the standing rib itself. Serve for the family **only** since you may be tempted to growl a bit. Very tasty.*

Eye of Round Roast with Marinade

Prepare roast 1 day in advance of serving.

½ cup soy sauce
½ cup dry vermouth
2 garlic cloves, minced
1 teaspoon dry mustard
1 teaspoon ground ginger

1 teaspoon thyme (optional)
4 to 5 pound eye of round roast
1 cup water
2 pounds small fresh mushrooms

Combine soy sauce, vermouth, garlic, mustard, ginger, and thyme; mix well. Place the eye of round roast into a glass dish the size of the roast, and pour the marinade over it. Cover, and refrigerate overnight, turning occasionally to marinate all sides evenly. About 3½ hours before serving time, remove roast from the refrigerator to allow roast to warm to room temperature for 1 hour before cooking time. Preheat oven to 500°. Pour marinade off roast and reserve. Place roast in a pan on a rack, fat side on top, and add water to pan. Bake uncovered for 3 to 4 minutes per pound in the preheated oven. At end of cooking time, turn oven off; and allow roast to remain in the hot oven for 2 hours. Do not open the oven door. Roast will be rare to medium rare. Add some of the reserved marinade to the natural juices of the roast, and slice the mushrooms into the gravy. Cook mushrooms in the gravy for about 5 minutes. Serve hot mushroom gravy over the roast slices.

Five Hundred Degree Roast

Sirloin tip or rump roast
Soy sauce
Salt

Coarse black pepper
2-4 cups water

Preheat oven to 500°. Bring roast to room temperature; then place in an open baking pan or iron skillet. Liberally shake on soy sauce, letting some collect in the bottom of the pan. Salt lightly all over, allowing for the salt content in the soy, and pepper fairly heavily. Add water to pan. Place, uncovered, in the preheated oven, and cook for 7 minutes per pound; turn oven off, and do not open oven door for 2 hours. The roast at serving time will be pink and delicious.

Spicy Corned Beef

When selecting a corned beef, get the leanest one available; also buy a large one since they "shrink." There are three methods to cook a corned beef to preserve the flavor that is lost if it is boiled.

All methods: if pickling spices are not on beef when purchased, add 2 tablespoons crab boil or pickling spices on the top surface of the beef.

To microwave: place corned beef in an oven cooking bag. Secure the end with the non-metallic tie wrap, and pierce the top of the bag 6 times. Place bag with beef in it in a glass baking dish in the microwave. Cook on setting 7 (on a 1-10 scale) for 3 minutes per pound; then on setting 4 for 10 minutes per pound. Serve hot or allow to cool, and wrap in plastic wrap and foil before refrigerating.

To cook in oven: wrap corned beef in heavy foil, and place, seam-side up, in an open roasting pan or iron skillet. Bake at 350° for 2 hours; then open foil to expose beef, and continue cooking for another 2 hours. Serve hot or allow to cool, and wrap in plastic wrap and foil before refrigerating.

To cook on the grill: wrap corned beef in heavy foil and place, seam-side up, in an aluminum pie pan over indirect heat. Close top of grill, with all vents open. Cook 2 hours; then open foil to expose beef, and cook another 2 hours. Serve hot or allow to cool, and wrap in plastic wrap and foil before refrigerating.

Corned beef seems to have the best flavor when sliced thin. It is also great for an appetizer. Serve on party rye with a good, hot mustard.

Old World Brisket

Prepare 1 day before serving.

4	tablespoons coarse ground black pepper	½	cup vinegar
1	(4-pound) boneless brisket	1	tablespoon tomato sauce
⅔	cup soy sauce	1	teaspoon paprika
		1	medium clove garlic, minced

Spread black pepper on brisket, and press into the meat, coating the entire surface of the brisket. Place brisket in a glass casserole just large enough to hold brisket and marinade. Combine soy sauce, vinegar, tomato sauce, paprika, and garlic; mix well. Carefully spoon the sauce over the peppered brisket to avoid loosening the pepper. Cover and refrigerate overnight; turn once. When ready to cook, remove from sauce, and wrap tightly in heavy aluminum foil. Place in a pan, and bake at 300° for 4 hours. Serve hot and sliced very thin, or cool and refrigerate; then slice very thin. Serves 8.

Outstanding as a hot entrée, a cold appetizer, or a cold sandwich. Regardless of how it is served, slice very thin to enhance the flavor.

Savory Roast

Salt and pepper for roast		4	tablespoons Worcestershire sauce
1	(3 to 4-pound) roast, less tender cuts may be used	4	tablespoons soy sauce
2	tablespoons vegetable oil	1	teaspoon garlic salt
½	cup catsup	¼	teaspoon dry mustard
½	cup vinegar		

Lightly salt and pepper the roast. In an electric skillet, sear roast in the hot oil until browned on all sides. In a saucepan, combine all other ingredients, and bring to a boil. Pour hot sauce over the hot roast; cover and simmer for 1-1½ hours or until tender.

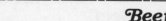

Oriental Roast

1   (4-pound) roast, less tender
    cuts may be used
Salt for roast
2   tablespoons vegetable oil
¼   teaspoon pepper
¼   cup soy sauce
1   tablespoon honey

1½ teaspoons celery seed
1   teaspoon garlic salt
¼   teaspoon dry mustard
1   cup water
1   tablespoon vinegar
½   teaspoon ground ginger
2   tablespoons cornstarch

Lightly salt roast on all sides. In an electric skillet, heat oil on high, and sear the roast until browned on all sides. Mix all other ingredients except the cornstarch in a separate saucepan, and bring to a boil. Pour hot sauce over the hot roast; cover, and reduce heat to simmer. Cook until roast is very tender. Thicken the gravy with the cornstarch mixed with ¼ cup cold water. Serves 8.

Braised Beef Short Ribs with Horseradish Sauce

Salt and pepper
3   pounds beef short ribs, cut
    apart
Vegetable oil
1   medium onion, chopped
2   ribs celery, chopped

4   whole cloves
1   large clove garlic, minced
1   cup sour cream
1   cup beef stock
2   tablespoons horseradish

Salt and pepper the ribs; then brown on all sides in a small amount of vegetable oil in a hot skillet. Add onion, celery, cloves, and garlic; stir to mix. Reduce heat to simmer; cover and cook for ½ hour or until tender. Remove whole cloves. Combine sour cream, beef stock, and horseradish. Pour sauce over the ribs, and stir. Do not allow the mixture to boil after adding the sour cream. Simmer for 10 minutes, uncovered. Serves 4.

Stuffed Round Steak

1½ cups soft bread crumbs
2   tablespoons grated onion
1   tablespoon parsley, chopped
1   teaspoon salt

¼   teaspoon pepper
1   small clove garlic, minced
¼   cup water
1   round steak, ½-inch thick

Combine bread crumbs, onion, parsley, salt, pepper, and garlic. Moisten with the water, and mix well. Spread the stuffing over the surface of the steak. Roll steak with stuffing on the inside, and tie with a heavy string wound diagonally around length of steak to secure. In an electric skillet, slowly brown the steak on all sides in a small amount of vegetable oil. Add ¼-½ cup of water; cover, and simmer until tender, about 1½ hours. Remove string to slice.

French Steak

Salt and pepper
1½ pounds round steak, cut into
    6-8 serving pieces
¼   cup plain flour
3   tablespoons vegetable oil
1   clove garlic, minced

½   cup green onions, chopped
1   (10½-ounce) can consommé
2   tablespoons sour cream
½   teaspoon paprika
Hot rice

Salt and pepper the steak pieces; then coat with the flour. In a skillet, heat oil, and brown the steak on all sides. Remove steak from the skillet, and keep warm. Add garlic and onions to the skillet; cook until tender. Return steak to the skillet, and add consommé. Cover and cook on simmer for 30 minutes. Uncover and stir in the sour cream and paprika. Simmer another 10 minutes; do not allow mixture to boil after adding sour cream. Serve over hot rice. Serves 4 to 6.

Country Fried Steak

2   pounds round steak, ½ inch
    thick
Salt and pepper
½   cup plain flour

Vegetable oil
2   large onions, sliced
1   cup water
¼   teaspoon paprika

Cut steak into 6 serving pieces. Salt and pepper each piece, and coat with the flour. In a large skillet or electric skillet, heat oil and brown coated steak on all sides. Place onions on top of steak. Add water and paprika to the skillet. Reduce heat to simmer, and cover. Cook for about 30 minutes or until steak is tender. Add more water, if needed. Serves 6.

Baked Steak Parmesan

½   cup Parmesan cheese, grated
½   cup dry bread crumbs
1   pound round steak, cut into
    serving size pieces
1   egg, well beaten
Salt and pepper
3   tablespoons vegetable oil,
    more if needed

1   medium onion, chopped
2   tablespoons margarine
1½ cups tomato sauce
1¾ cups hot water
¼   teaspoon crushed oregano
10 ounces sliced Mozzarella
    cheese

Mix Parmesan cheese and bread crumbs. Dip steak pieces into egg; then salt and pepper. Coat steak pieces with the cheese and crumb mixture. In a skillet, heat oil, and fry coated steak until browned. In a separate skillet, sauté onions in the margarine until limp. Add tomato sauce, hot water, and oregano. Bring to a boil for 2 minutes; remove from heat. In a flat greased casserole, place a layer of sauce, layer of steak, the Mozzarella cheese, and the remaining sauce. Bake uncovered at 350° for 30 minutes. Serves 6.

A Little Cuban Cube Steak

Vegetable oil	½ fresh lime for each steak
Cube steaks	Chopped green onion
Salt and pepper	Chopped fresh parsley

In a skillet, heat a little oil on high; add cube steaks, and reduce heat slightly. Pan fry steaks until just done; then salt and pepper. Remove to a heated platter, and squeeze lime over each steak; then top with green onions and parsley.

The Cubans use a cut of meat that they pound vigorously with a mallet. The cube steak is a reasonable substitute, and the overall effect is "muy bueno."

Sirloin Beef-Ka-Bobs

Marinate beef overnight.

1 (3-pound) sirloin tip roast	1 teaspoon garlic salt
1 (15-ounce) bottle Worcestershire sauce	2 drops Tabasco sauce
1 pound margarine, melted	Vegetables of choice for Ka-Bobs

Cut roast into large cubes for skewers. Combine Worcestershire sauce, melted margarine, garlic salt, and Tabasco sauce in a glass bowl large enough to hold the sirloin cubes. Add cubes to the marinade, tossing well to coat all the cubes; then cover bowl, and refrigerate overnight. When ready to use, thread cubes onto the skewers alternating with vegetables. Grill slowly over coals until sirloin and vegetables are tender. Remove from skewers and serve. Serves 6.

Beef San Simeon

1 pound round steak
1 cup water
⅓ cup tarragon vinegar
1 small onion, minced
½ teaspoon black pepper
Scant ¼ teaspoon red pepper
12 ounces linguine
Salt
4 tablespoons margarine
4 teaspoons cornstarch

1 large clove garlic, minced
2 tablespoons vegetable oil
1 (16-ounce) package frozen broccoli, cauliflower, and carrots
1 large onion, sliced in rings
2 cups fresh mushrooms, sliced
Parmesan cheese, grated

Partially freeze beef; slice in thin strips. Combine water, vinegar, the small onion, black pepper, and red pepper. Add beef; toss to coat beef strips with marinade. Allow beef to stand in marinade at room temperature for 15 minutes. Cook linguine according to package directions in salted water; drain. Toss drained linguine with the margarine; cover and place over hot water to keep warm. Drain beef, reserving the marinade. Stir cornstarch into the marinade, and set aside. In a large skillet or Dutch oven, sauté the garlic in the vegetable oil for 1 minute. Add beef, and stir-fry until beef looses red color. Salt beef to taste. Remove beef, and keep warm. Add frozen broccoli, cauliflower, and carrots; stir-fry for 4 minutes. Add onion rings; stir-fry for 2 minutes. Add mushrooms; stir-fry 1 minute. Stir in marinade mixture and beef; cook over medium heat until hot and slightly thickened. Add salt if needed. Serve over the hot linguine, and sprinkle with Parmesan cheese. Serves 6 to 8.

Cajun Grillades

1 (1 pound) round steak, cut very thin (⅛ to ¼ inch thick)
½ teaspoon garlic powder
¼ teaspoon garlic salt
¼ teaspoon onion salt
¼ teaspoon cayenne pepper
½ cup plain flour
2 tablespoons vegetable oil, more if needed

Cut the steak into about 8 small pieces, and pound with a mallet or rolling pin until very thin. In a bowl, combine garlic powder, garlic salt, onion salt, cayenne pepper, and flour; mix well. Sprinkle the pounded steak with extra garlic salt, a little extra garlic powder, and a very little extra cayenne pepper. Dredge the seasoned steak pieces in the seasoned flour to coat. Heat oil until hot, but not smoking, and quickly brown the grillades while stirring; serve hot. Serves 2 to 4.

Beef with Mushroom Caps

¼ cup margarine
1½ pounds tender beef, cut in ½ inch strips
1 large onion, minced
1 small clove garlic, minced
8 ounces button mushrooms, drained
2 tablespoons plain flour
2 (10½-ounce) cans consommé
1 teaspoon Worcestershire sauce
⅛ teaspoon pepper
Salt to taste
Hot rice or noodles

In a skillet, melt margarine, and sauté beef strips until browned on all sides. Remove beef; add onions, garlic, and mushrooms to the skillet. Sauté until onions are tender. Stir in the flour, and gradually add the consommé. Cook over medium heat, while stirring, until thickened. Add Worcestershire sauce and pepper; return beef strips to skillet and stir. Salt to taste. Cover skillet, and simmer for about 30 minutes or until beef is tender. Serve over hot rice or noodles. Serves 4.

Betty's Baked Lasagna

Sauce:

3 pounds ground chuck	2 (15-ounce) cans tomato sauce
2 cups onions, chopped	1 tablespoon oregano, crushed
2 cloves garlic, minced	2 teaspoons onion or garlic salt
2 teaspoons MSG	¼ teaspoon pepper
3 teaspoons salt, divided	
2 (28-ounce) cans tomatoes, chopped	

Layers:

1½ pounds lasagna noodles	3 (6-ounce) packages sliced Mozzarella cheese
4 eggs, well beaten	1 cup Parmesan cheese, grated
3 pounds cottage cheese	

Directions for sauce:

In a Dutch oven, brown chuck, onions, and garlic, crumbling the meat while cooking. Add MSG and 1 teaspoon of the salt; mix well. Add tomatoes, tomato sauce, remaining 2 teaspoons salt, oregano, onion (or garlic) salt, and pepper. Stir very well, and bring to a boil; then reduce heat to simmer. Cook, uncovered, for 2½ hours. Do not cut the cooking time. Skim off any extra grease from the top of the pot.

Directions for layers:

Cook lasagna noodles in a large pot of boiling, salted water with a little oil added to the water. When water is boiling, add noodles one at a time; cook, covered, for 15-20 minutes. Be careful not to overcook noodles; they should be just tender — al dente. Immediately drain noodles, and separate onto waxed paper to keep them from wedding. In a large bowl, beat eggs, and add cottage cheese; mix very well. Remove Mozzarella cheese slices from packages, and stack on top of each other; then slice diagonally three times. Lightly grease two 9×13×2 inch baking dishes. Begin layers with a thin layer of meat sauce, just covering bottom of dish. Cover meat sauce with a layer of noodles that barely overlap. Next, add ¼ of the cottage cheese mixture; then ¼ of the Mozzarella diagonal slices, spaced evenly. Top with ¼ of the Parmesan cheese. Repeat layers of meat sauce, noodles, cottage cheese, Mozzarella, and Parmesan; then assemble the second dish. Bake uncovered on a cookie sheet in a preheated oven at 350° for 50 minutes. Remove from the oven, and let stand at least 10 minutes before cutting into squares. Serves 12 to 16.

(Continued next page)

Baked Lasagna is perfect for a casual dinner. It can be prepared three days in advance and refrigerated, or it can be frozen. Only the baking time is required when serving, so there's plenty of time for conversation. Add a large, beautiful bowl of cold, fresh fruit and lots of hot, buttered French or Italian bread. There'll be requests for seconds and hints for another invitation. I prefer to make the sauce one day, then assemble the layers on the following day. All of this chatter sounds so cool and graceful; did I fail to mention that your kitchen may look like a war zone or that once I mistook Comet for the Parmesan cheese? No doubt, my best batch to date!

Hot 'N Spicy Beef Roll

Beef Roll:

2	pounds lean ground beef	2	tablespoons Worcestershire sauce
1	teaspoon whole mustard seed	½	teaspoon garlic powder
1	tablespoon onion salt	1	teaspoon chives or onion flakes
1	tablespoon coarse black pepper	1	teaspoon salt
			Dash chili powder

Sauce:

2	tablespoons margarine	1	tablespoon parsley
1	tablespoon plain flour	2	teaspoons Worcestershire sauce
1	(10½-ounce) can consommé		

Allow ground beef to come to room temperature; then add all beef roll ingredients, and mix thoroughly. Form into a long roll, and place in a greased baking dish. Make diagonal indentions on top of the roll, about 1 inch apart, to hold a little sauce. In a skillet, melt margarine, and add flour. Stir to form a smooth paste; then gradually add undiluted consommé. Stir in parsley and Worcestershire sauce, and cook slowly until thickened. Put sauce aside to use halfway through cooking time. Bake beef roll at 350° for 20 minutes; then remove from oven, and spoon off excess fat. Pour sauce over top of beef roll; return to oven, and continue to cook for 20 minutes longer. Remove from oven, and again spoon off any excess fat, leaving the gravy. Let beef roll cool for a few minutes; then slice, and serve over hot rice with the gravy. Serves 5 to 6.

Oriental Chi Chow

1	pound sirloin steak, 1-inch thick	½	cup green onions, sliced
2	tablespoons peanut oil	1	medium onion, sliced in thin rings
1	pint fresh mushrooms, sliced	½	cup condensed beef broth
1	(5-ounce) can bamboo shoots, drained	2	teaspoons cornstarch
1	(16-ounce) can bean sprouts, drained	1	tablespoon cold water
1	(5-ounce) can water chestnuts, drained and sliced	¼	cup soy sauce
		1	pinch sugar
			Chow mein noodles or hot rice

Partially freeze steak; then slice into thin strips. Arrange ingredients on an attractive tray; then cook the oriental way, at the table. Brown steak in hot oil in an electric skillet or electric wok. Cover the skillet, letting the steak simmer for 5 minutes. Add mushrooms, bamboo shoots, bean sprouts, water chestnuts, green onions, onion rings, beef broth, and simmer, covered, for 7 minutes. Blend cornstarch, water, soy sauce, and sugar; then stir into the skillet, and quickly coat all ingredients as the sauce thickens. Serve over chow mein noodles or hot rice. Serves 4 to 5.

This dish is very festive. It not only gives you a culinary treat, but entertains the adults and fascinates the children!

Helen's Beef and Peppers with Rice

1½ pounds round or boneless sirloin steak, partially frozen
½ cup margarine
1 large onion, sliced in rings
1 medium green pepper, cut in thin strips
Salt and pepper to taste
Soy sauce to taste
Hot rice

Slice the partially frozen beef into thin strips. In a large skillet, heat margarine to high, and quickly stir-fry the beef strips, onion rings, and green pepper strips until beef has lost red color. Add salt, pepper, and soy sauce to taste. Serve over hot rice. Serves 3 to 4.

Beef Enchiladas

Sauce:

2 medium onions, minced
3 tablespoons vegetable oil
¼ cup chili powder
23 ounces tomato sauce
3 small cloves garlic, minced
¾ teaspoon oregano

¾ teaspoon ground cumin
1½ teaspoons salt
2 tablespoons sugar
1 tablespoon cocoa (do not omit)

Filling:

1½ pounds lean ground beef
1 large onion, chopped
1 (15-ounce) can refried beans
1 teaspoon salt
1 clove garlic, minced
⅓ cup hot taco sauce

Vegetable oil
12 frozen corn tortillas, thawed
3 cups sharp Cheddar cheese, grated
Sour cream (optional)
Black olives (optional)

Sauce directions:
Sauté onion in the oil until limp. Add chili powder, and cook on medium heat for 1 minute. Add remaining sauce ingredients; bring to a boil. Reduce heat to simmer, and cook, covered, for 20 minutes. Stir sauce frequently. Set sauce aside.

Filling directions:
Sauté beef and onions until beef is browned; drain off fat. Stir in beans, salt, garlic, and taco sauce. Set aside. In a small skillet, cover the bottom with a small amount of vegetable oil. Heat oil on low to just soften tortillas, do **not** fry. Slip tortillas into oil one at a time, until soft. Remove tortillas with tongs to absorbent paper towel.

To assemble:
In a greased 9 × 13 inch baking dish, pour a layer of the sauce. Fill each tortilla with the beef mixture, and roll. Place rolled enchiladas with seam side down in the sauce. Pour remaining sauce over the enchiladas, and top with the cheese. Bake at 350° for only 15 minutes; immediately remove from the oven. Keep warm on a warming tray, if needed. Serve topped with sour cream and black olive slices, if desired. Serves 6.

Chili

2 pounds lean ground beef	2 teaspoons salt
1½ cups onion, chopped	1 tablespoon ground cumin
2 cloves garlic, minced	1 tablespoon sugar
4 tablespoons chili powder	2 cups water
2 tablespoons plain flour	16 ounces tomato sauce
2 teaspoons cocoa (do not omit)	Cooked beans, if desired

In a Dutch oven, brown beef and drain; then add onion and garlic, and cook until onion is limp. Stir in the remaining ingredients, except beans, and mix well. Cover and simmer 30 to 45 minutes. Add beans and cook 5-10 minutes longer. Serves 6 to 8.

Chinese Stew

2 pounds beef stew meat	2 tablespoons soy sauce
½ teaspoon pepper	1 small head cabbage, cut into 1-inch pieces
1 tablespoon vegetable oil	
1 (10¾-ounce) can golden mushroom soup	1 (5-ounce) can bamboo shoots, drained and cut in half
1¼ cups water	
1 onion, thinly sliced	

Sprinkle meat with pepper; then brown in hot oil in an electric skillet or heavy pot. Add soup, water, onion, and soy; then cover and simmer for 1½ hours or until tender. Add cabbage and bamboo shoots. Simmer, covered, for 8 minutes longer. Serves 6.

Ground Beef Stroganoff

2½ pounds ground beef, cooked and drained
1 teaspoon salt
3 medium onions, chopped
4 ounces mushrooms, sliced or chopped
3 (10½-ounce) cans beef consommé
1 drop Tabasco sauce

2 teaspoons Worcestershire sauce
1 clove garlic, minced
2 tablespoons cornstarch
¼ cup cold water
2 ounces sour cream
Hot rice
Paprika

In a Dutch oven, combine cooked beef, salt, onions, mushrooms, consommé, Tabasco, Worcestershire, and garlic. Bring to a boil; cover, and reduce heat to simmer. Cook for about 30 minutes. Mix cornstarch with cold water, and stir into Stroganoff. Stir until thickened; then remove from heat. Gradually add the sour cream. Do not allow Stroganoff to come to a boil after sour cream has been added. Serve over hot rice with paprika sprinkled to garnish. Serves 6 to 8.

Beef Patties Consommé

6 beef patties
1 (10½-ounce) can consommé
1 tablespoon parsley
1 teaspoon margarine

2 teaspoons Worcestershire sauce
1 tablespoon cornstarch
½ cup water

In a skillet, cook beef patties until browned on both sides; drain all excess fat. Add consommé, parsley, margarine, and Worcestershire sauce. Cover and simmer for about 15 minutes. Combine cornstarch and water; then pour into the skillet. Stir, while cooking, to thicken the gravy. Remove from heat. Serve over hot rice or creamed potatoes. Serves 4 to 6.

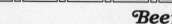
True French Canadian Tourtière by Elaine

2 pounds beef, minced	Pepper to taste
2 pounds pork, minced	Thyme to taste
2 pounds veal, minced	4 pounds raw potatoes, peeled
2 large onions, minced	and minced
Salt to taste	Pastry

Combine all the meats with the onions, salt, pepper, and thyme; mix very well. Stir potatoes into the meat mixture. Place the mixture into 1 large greased casserole or 2 smaller greased casseroles. Top with a layer of pastry. Pierce top of pastry in an attractive design to allow steam to escape. Bake at 325° for 4 hours. If pastry should brown too fast, cover loosely with aluminum foil. Serves 12 or more.

Our friend, Elaine, from the beautiful Canadian city of Ottawa, sent this favorite French Canadian recipe. It is very hearty and well-suited to a climate where people need to put "a little meat on their bones" for the cold, snowy winters.

Bacon and Beef Steak Wrappers

1 pound ground chuck	3 tablespoons stuffed green
½ teaspoon garlic salt	olives, sliced
¼ cup Parmesan cheese, grated	3 tablespoons green onions,
1 (2-ounce) can mushrooms	sliced
	6 slices bacon

Roll ground chuck with rolling pin on waxed paper into a 12×7 inch rectangle. Sprinkle with garlic salt and cheese. Combine chopped mushrooms, olives, and green onions, and sprinkle evenly on meat. Roll meat (by gently lifting waxed paper), jelly-roll style, and freeze until firm enough to slice. Cut into 6 pieces, and wrap each piece with a slice of bacon; secure with a toothpick. Cook on the grill for 10 minutes on each side. Serves 4 to 6.

Poultry

Chicken Cordon Bleu

6   chicken breast halves,
    skinned and boned
Salt and pepper
6   thin slices ham
3   slices Swiss cheese, halved

½   cup Ritz cracker crumbs
2   tablespoons Parmesan
    cheese, grated
2   tablespoons parsley, minced
¼   cup margarine, melted

Place chicken breasts on a cutting board; cover with waxed paper, and lightly pound to flatten the breasts. Do not cut through meat. Discard waxed paper. Lightly salt and pepper the breasts. Place a slice of ham and ½ slice of Swiss cheese on each breast. (Cheese may need to be folded to fit on breast.) Roll the breast, jelly roll style; secure with a toothpick. Combine cracker crumbs, Parmesan cheese, and parsley. Melt margarine, and dip rolled breasts in the margarine; then in the cracker crumb mixture. Place in a greased casserole. Bake at 350° for 45 minutes. Serves 6.

Chicken Clarisse

1   chicken fryer, cut into pieces
1   cup apricot preserves
½   small onion, minced

½   teaspoon garlic salt
½   cup barbecue sauce
2   tablespoons soy sauce

Place the chicken pieces into a well-greased baking dish. Mix together all other ingredients, and spread over the chicken pieces. Bake, uncovered, at 350° for 1 hour and 15 minutes. Serves 4 to 6.

Jane's Poulet A L'Estragon

3 whole chicken breasts (6 halves), boned, skinned, and salted
1 onion, sliced thin
1 carrot, sliced thin
¼ teaspoon dry tarragon
½ cup dry white wine
3 tablespoons butter

3 tablespoons plain flour
½ teaspoon salt
Dash of pepper
1 egg yolk
3 tablespoons heavy cream or milk
Paprika

Place chicken, onion, carrot, tarragon, and wine in a large skillet or Dutch oven; add just enough water to cover the chicken (about 4 cups). Cover, and bring to a boil; then lower temperature, and simmer for 25 minutes or until tender. Remove chicken, and keep warm. Strain liquid; then cook over high heat until reduced to about 2 cups.

In a heavy saucepan, melt 3 tablespoons butter; stir in flour, salt, and pepper until smooth. Gradually add the 2 cups chicken broth, stirring to keep smooth. Cook over moderate heat until thickened. Combine egg yolk and cream; then blend into broth mixture while beating vigorously. Arrange the chicken breasts that have been kept warm on a serving platter, and pour the hot sauce over them. Garnish with paprika. Serves 4 to 6.

Wild Rice

¾ cup wild rice
3 cups boiling water

1 teaspoon salt
Butter

Wash the rice in 4 changes of cold water to clean. In a saucepan of 3 cups boiling water, add salt, and gradually stir in the rice to keep the water boiling. Cover and reduce heat to simmer. Stir occasionally with a fork. Cook for 30-45 minutes or until rice is tender and water is absorbed. Add butter and stir. Yield: 2¼ cups.

Hot white rice can be added to the wild rice to give a "softer" blend of textures.

Almand's Chicken Kiev

8   large chicken breast halves,
     skinned, boned, and salted
½   cup margarine, softened
2   tablespoons parsley, minced
2   tablespoons chives, minced
⅛   teaspoon garlic powder
½   teaspoon salt
½   teaspoon pepper

1   teaspoon Worcestershire
     sauce
1 or 2 eggs, as needed
½   cup milk (more may be
     needed)
Plain flour
Ritz cracker crumbs
Vegetable oil for frying

Place breast halves on a cutting board, and gently pound to flatten. Do not cut through meat. In a small bowl, cream margarine with parsley, chives, garlic powder, salt, pepper, and Worcestershire sauce. Worcestershire sauce will not completely mix with the margarine. Divide margarine mixture into 8 equal ovals. Place ovals on a cookie sheet, and freeze. When margarine ovals are hard, place in the center of breast fillets, and fold the meat to completely cover the margarine. Secure with toothpicks. In a small bowl, beat 1 egg with the milk (another egg and milk mixture may be required to complete batter process). Roll fillets in flour; dip in the egg mixture, and roll in cracker crumbs. Fry in deep oil at 360° for about 8 to 10 minutes until golden brown. Keep warm on a warming tray, uncovered, until serving time. Serves 8.

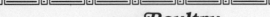

Chicken with Light Curry Sauce and "Side Boys"

Salt and pepper for chicken	¼ teaspoon curry powder
6 chicken breast halves, boned	½ cup chicken stock or broth
3 tablespoons margarine	½ cup milk
2 tablespoons plain flour	Hot rice
½ teaspoon salt	

Side Boys:

¾ cup cashews, chopped	6 green onions with tops,
¾ cup raisins	chopped
¾ cup soy mixture (½ cup soy sauce, ¼ cup dry white wine, 2 tablespoons toasted sesame seeds, 1 teaspoon peanut oil; mixed vigorously)	1 cup chutney (see Tomato Chutney)

Salt and pepper chicken breasts, and refrigerate for several hours. Cook chicken, uncovered, in oven at 350° for 45 minutes or until tender and done. In a skillet, melt margarine, and blend in flour and salt until smooth; then add curry powder and chicken stock, keeping the mixture smooth. Add milk, and heat on medium high, stirring constantly, until thickened.

Use small attractive bowls with demitasse spoons for the "Side Boys" and place on a tray. Serve the chicken breasts on a bed of hot rice topped with the Curry Sauce. Guests select condiment toppings from the "Side Boy" tray.

There are endless numbers of "Side Boys" to be used. In India, the importance of a guest is determined by the number of "Side Boys" served. Since your guests will be of great importance, here are more "Side Boys" to select from: Toasted, shaved coconut; crumbled bacon; currant jelly; thin slices of cucumber tossed in oil and vinegar with salt; thin slices of firm banana tossed in oil, vinegar, and coarse black pepper; Mandarin orange slices, well drained; chopped almonds and peanuts; etc. Serves 4 to 6.

Tomato Chutney

1	tablespoon vegetable oil	4	medium tomatoes, peeled and chopped
½	teaspoon cumin		
¼	teaspoon crushed red pepper	1	tablespoon lemon juice
½	teaspoon nutmeg	½	cup sugar
2	tablespoons mustard seeds	½	cup raisins

In a saucepan, heat oil, and add cumin, crushed red pepper, nutmeg, and mustard seeds. When mustard seeds begin to move in the skillet, add the tomatoes and lemon juice. Simmer, while stirring, for 15 minutes; then add sugar and the raisins. Simmer for 30 minutes more, stirring often, until mixture has thickened. When cooled, store in a tight jar in the refrigerator. Serve with the curry dinner at room temperature.

Baked Chicken Breasts Élégante

6	chicken breast halves	½	cup milk
Salt, pepper, and paprika		6-8	ounces mushrooms, drained
7	tablespoons margarine	1	(4½-ounce) jar cocktail onions, drained
1	tablespoon Worcestershire sauce		

Wash the chicken breasts, and pat dry. Sprinkle breasts with salt, pepper, and paprika. Melt margarine in a skillet, and brown the breasts. Remove breasts to a greased casserole. Allow margarine left in the skillet to cool; then add Worcestershire sauce and the milk. Stir well; add mushrooms and onions. Pour the mixture over the chicken breasts and cover. Bake at 325° for 1 hour or until tender. Serve over a combination of white rice and wild rice. Serves 3 to 6.

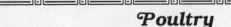

Breast of Chicken Wellington

Prepare chicken breasts 1 day before serving.

1 (6-ounce) box of long grain and wild rice mix	1 package Pillsbury All Ready Pie Crusts (2 crusts folded in the package)
6 chicken breast halves, skinned and boned	6 ounces red currant jelly
Seasoned salt	½ teaspoon Dijon mustard
Pepper	1 tablespoon orange juice
1 egg white	1 tablespoon cooking sherry

Cook rice according to directions on the box; set aside to cool. Flatten the chicken by lightly pounding; sprinkle with salt and pepper. Beat the egg white until soft peaks form. Add 1½ cups of the cooked rice mixture to the egg white; mix well. cut 6 quarters from the pastry. Place each quarter on a floured board and roll larger. Place a breast in the center of each pastry, and add about ¼ cup of the rice mixture on the breast. Roll pastry and chicken over the rice, jelly roll style. (The rolled package will look like an eggroll.) Seal ends of pastry to contain the rice. Place seam side down in a greased baking pan. Cover and refrigerate overnight. When ready to serve, preheat oven to 375°; remove baking pan from refrigerator, and immediately place into the preheated oven. Bake uncovered for 35 to 45 minutes. If pastry begins to brown too fast, loosely cover with a piece of aluminum foil. While chicken is cooking, place the jelly in a saucepan, and melt. Stir in mustard, orange juice, and sherry; heat. Serve the hot sauce over the hot pastry-covered chicken. Serves 6.

Coat of Arms Chicken Breasts

4 chicken breast halves	4 green pepper rings
Salt and pepper	4 slices bacon
4 thick slices of onion	2 tablespoons vegetable oil

Wash chicken breast halves, and pat dry; salt and pepper. Place an onion slice on the meaty side of the breast; then fit the green pepper ring around the outside of the onion. Attach bacon slice with a toothpick to the backside of the breast; then stretch the slice around breast to make a crisscross over the onion slice. Attach end of bacon with a toothpick to backside of breast. Place breasts in the hot vegetable oil, meaty side down; reduce heat, and fry until bacon is crisp and brown. Turn breasts over, and cook until very tender. Serves 4.

Chicken Diane

6 chicken breast halves	2 tablespoons cooking sherry
Salt and pepper	1 (10¾-ounce) can cream of
6 tablespoons margarine	mushroom soup
½ cup sour cream	

Salt and pepper breasts. In a skillet, melt margarine, and brown breasts on all sides. Place browned breasts in a greased casserole. Add sour cream, sherry, and cream of mushroom soup to the margarine in the skillet; mix well. Pour the sauce over the breasts, and cover the casserole. Bake at 350° for about 1 hour or until tender. Serves 6.

Roasted Stuffed Chicken

1 fryer, 3 to 3½ pounds	4 tablespoons hot bacon drippings or hot oil, divided
Salt and pepper	
1 cup self-rising corn meal	1 egg, beaten
½ medium onion, chopped	3 slices raw bacon
¾ cup buttermilk	

Salt and pepper fryer over entire surface and inside the cavity; set aside. In a bowl, combine corn meal, onion, and buttermilk; mix well. In a non-stick skillet, heat the 4 tablespoons of drippings until hot, but not smoking. Pour 2 tablespoons of the hot drippings into the batter, and beat vigorously. Add beaten egg, and blend well. Pour batter into the remaining hot drippings in the skillet. Cook over medium heat, and stir until the stuffing mixture is cooked and crumbled. Stuff the fryer cavity with the hot stuffing. Place the stuffed fryer in a greased baking pan, and crisscross the slices of raw bacon over the breast. Bake at 350° for 1¾ to 2 hours. If bacon begins to brown too fast, place a loose sheet of aluminum foil over the breast. Serves 4 to 6.

Use the same recipe if stuffing Cornish hens. Place 1 slice of bacon, folded into a V-shape, over each hen's breast. Wrap hens in aluminum foil, and bake 1½ hours. Open foil, and bake another 20 minutes.

Crusty Brown Whole Baked Chicken

1 (3-3½ pound) chicken fryer

Place whole chicken with breast side up in a greased 2 quart baking dish with nothing on it and no liquid added. Bake at 350° for about 2 hours. Remove from oven, and immediately salt and pepper the chicken over the entire surface. The hot meat will draw in the salt. Carve and serve while still hot. Serves 4 to 6.

The simplest possible way to cook a chicken, but so very delicious. Chicken stays moist on the inside, but crusty on the outside.

Georgia's Best Baked Chicken

1 chicken fryer, cut in pieces	Paprika
Salt	Margarine
Pepper	Water
Plain flour	

Place chicken pieces in a greased 3-quart baking dish; then salt, pepper, and spoon flour generously on all pieces. Turn chicken over in the dish, and repeat; then spinkle with paprika. Dot the pieces of chicken with margarine, using as much or as little as desired. Being careful not to wash off the flour coating on top of the chicken, pour water into baking dish until baking dish is ½ full. Bake uncovered at 350° for 1½ to 2 hours or until chicken is very tender. Baste with pan juices once or twice during the cooking time to moisten any flour that appears dry. Serves 4 to 6.

Georgia was a "member" of our family for many years, cooking for both my mother and my grandmother at different times. As a young girl, I deviled her endlessly to teach me to cook. She good-naturedly put up with me, and taught me many of her grand recipes.

Chicken Hong Kong

1 chicken fryer, cut in pieces	¼ cup soy sauce
1 teaspoon garlic powder	1 cup water
¼ teaspoon pepper	2 tablespoons cornstarch
¼ cup margarine	¼ cup cold water (for
Juice of 1½ lemons	cornstarch)

Dust chicken pieces with garlic powder and pepper. In an electric skillet, melt margarine, and brown chicken on all sides; remove pieces from skillet. Add lemon juice, soy, and water to skillet, and bring to a boil. Return chicken to skillet; cover, and reduce heat to simmer. Cook for 1 hour or until chicken is tender. Thicken gravy with the cornstarch dissolved in the ¼ cup water. Serves 4 to 6.

Barbecued Chicken

2½ to 3 pound chicken fryers, split in half	Salt and pepper
	1 recipe barbecue sauce

Plan on serving a quarter chicken per person with extra quarters for those who can't resist another bite. Do not quarter chickens until almost finished cooking.

Salt and pepper chicken halves 1 hour to 1 day before cooking, and refrigerate. Build a **medium** fire on one side of a covered-type grill. Allow grey ash to cover coals. Do not spread coals; leave them in a pile. Place chicken halves skin side down on the grill on **opposite** side from the fire. Do not allow any chicken to have direct fire under it. Cover grill, leaving all vents open. Cook for about 1½ to 1¾ hours, checking from time to time. Gently divide the halves into quarters, and dip the whole quarters into the barbecue sauce. Return to grill for about 10 to 15 minutes more. Chicken will be very tender and moist.

Have the fire the correct size and the chickens placed away from coals; then chickens will cook themselves. Great for having guests on the patio for dinner. Only a small amount of time is required to check on the grill, and the aroma will whet every appetite.

Barbecue Sauce Pfeiffer Style

½ cup vinegar
1 cup water
1 cup margarine
4 tablespoons sugar
2 tablespoons prepared mustard
1 onion, minced
1 teaspoon salt

1 teaspoon pepper
2 drops Tabasco sauce (more, if desired)
1½ lemons, sliced
1 cup catsup
4 tablespoons Worcestershire sauce

In a saucepan, combine vinegar, water, margarine, sugar, mustard, onion, salt, pepper, Tabasco, and lemon slices, and bring to a boil. Reduce heat, and simmer for 30 minutes. Add catsup and Worcestershire sauce, stir, and remove from heat. Use on chicken, ribs, pork chops, etc.

The sauce is tart and tangy and should be basted on the meat in the last quarter of cooking time. Easier yet, leave sauce in saucepan and dip pieces of meat into the sauce. Coats very well and saves time.

Herb Sauce for Smoking a Turkey

½ cup margarine
1 medium onion, minced
2 teaspoons dried herbs for salad
3 tablespoons brown sugar

1 clove garlic, crushed
¾ cup tarragon vinegar
1 teaspoon salt
Black pepper to taste

Melt margarine, and add all other ingredients. Place a foil drip pan under the turkey, then brush with the herb sauce. Cover top of turkey with a foil drape. Baste with sauce often until done.

Don's Mexican Chicken

1 chicken fryer, cut in pieces and salted	2 cups sharp Cheddar cheese, grated
Taco sauce (hot, medium, or mild)	Tortilla chips, broken

Place chicken pieces in a greased casserole, and pour taco sauce over the chicken according to taste. Cover the casserole, and bake at 350° for 1 to 1½ hours. Uncover, and sprinkle cheese over top of chicken, and cover with broken tortilla chips. Bake uncovered until cheese is melted and chips are hot. Serves 4 to 6.

Chicken Mediterranean

1 large cooking bag	1 green pepper, sliced in rings
1 tablespoon plain flour	4 ounces mushrooms, sliced
3-3½ pound fryer, cut in pieces	¼ cup soy sauce
Salt to taste	2 tablespoons wine vinegar
1 tablespoon paprika	1 clove garlic, crushed
1 medium onion, sliced	⅛ teaspoon oregano

Shake the flour inside the cooking bag to coat inside of bag, and place bag in a baking pan. Salt chicken pieces; then place pieces into the bag. Sprinkle paprika over top of chicken and arrange onion slices and green pepper rings on the chicken. Combine mushrooms, soy sauce, wine vinegar, garlic, and oregano. Pour mushroom mixture over the chicken. Close bag and secure with tie wrap provided with the cooking bag. Puncture top of bag 6 times to allow steam to escape. Bake at 350° for 1 to 1½ hours or until chicken is tender. Serves 4 to 6.

A Tart Little Chicken

1 chicken fryer, cut in pieces	¼ cup Worcestershire sauce
Salt and pepper	¼ cup catsup
¼ cup margarine	1 large clove garlic, crushed
¼ cup lemon juice	½ large onion, chopped
¼ cup vinegar	

Salt and pepper chicken pieces, and place in a flat, greased baking dish. Combine all other ingredients, and pour over the chicken pieces. Bake at 350° for about 1½ hours or until chicken is very tender. Serves 4 to 6.

Chicken Paprika

2 chicken fryers, cut in pieces	1 cup mushrooms, sliced
1 lemon, halved	2 tablespoons paprika
Salt to sprinkle on fryers	3 tablespoons plain flour
¼ cup margarine, divided	1 tablespoon catsup
2 tablespoons vegetable oil, divided	1½ teaspoons salt
½ cup onions, sliced thin	¼ teaspoon pepper
½ cup carrots, sliced thin	1 (10½-ounce) can chicken broth
½ cup celery, sliced thin	½ cup sour cream

Rub chicken with lemon halves while squeezing the lemon; then sprinkle with salt. Heat ½ of the margarine and ½ of the oil in a Dutch oven; brown chicken. Add remaining margarine and oil as needed. Remove chicken pieces as they brown. When all chicken is removed, add onions, carrots, celery, and mushrooms; sauté until slightly tender. Stir in the paprika, and cook for 1 minute; remove from heat. Then stir in flour, catsup, salt, and pepper. Gradually add chicken broth, and bring mixture to a boil, while stirring. Reduce heat, and simmer for 10 minutes; then add browned chicken. Simmer, covered, for 35 to 40 minutes or until chicken is tender. Remove chicken from sauce, and stir in sour cream. Heat sauce, but do not boil. Add chicken, and keep warm until served. Serves 8.

Serve Chicken Paprika with rice or noodles covered with the sauce. "Most too good!"

Chicken Easy

Salt and pepper
1 chicken fryer, cut in quarters
¼ cup margarine

2 large onions, sliced in rings
Chopped fresh parsley

Salt and pepper the chicken on all surfaces. In a large skillet or electric skillet, melt margarine, and brown chicken on all sides. Place onion rings on top of chicken. Cover skillet with a tight-fitting lid. Bring chicken to a boil; then reduce heat to simmer. Cook for 1 hour, turning chicken once after ½ hour of cooking time. Serve with chopped parsley on top of chicken and onions. Serves 4.

Chicken Colorado

1⅓ cups cooked rice
1½ cups green peppers, coarsely
    chopped
¾ cup thinly sliced onions
3 tablespoons vegetable oil
¼ cup cornstarch

2 cups chicken stock
3 tablespoons soy sauce
2 cups chicken, chopped
3 ripe tomatoes, peeled and
    cut in thin wedges

Cook rice, and keep warm. In a skillet, sauté green peppers and onions in the oil until just tender. In a small cup, mix cornstarch with a small amount of the chicken stock, and stir until smooth. Add cornstarch mixture to the skillet, and the remaining chicken stock. Stir in the soy sauce, and chicken. Cook over medium heat, while stirring, until the mixture has thickened. Add the tomatoes, and cook only long enough to heat. Serve hot over the rice. Serves 4-6.

Old South Chicken Pie

1	whole fryer, 3 pounds	2	cups chicken stock or broth
4	tablespoons margarine	2	tablespoons milk or cream
2	heaping tablespoons plain flour	2	hard-boiled eggs, peeled and chopped
1	teaspoon salt	2	unbaked deep-dish pie shells
¼	teaspoon pepper		

Boil chicken in salted water. When chicken is very tender, remove from stock, reserving the stock. Cool, and take meat off the bones. Cut chicken meat into bite-size pieces. In a skillet, melt the margarine; add flour, salt, pepper, and stir. Slowly add chicken stock, stirring to keep mixture smooth; then add milk. Cook, stirring constantly, until sauce thickens. Remove from heat, and add cut chicken and chopped egg; mix well. Remove one pie crust from its pan; thaw, flatten, and cut into strips. Pour chicken mixture into the remaining pie crust, and lattice the top with the pie crust strips. Bake at 350° for 35 minutes or until bubbling and golden brown on top. Serves 4 to 6.

Spicy Chicken and Pasta

12	ounces uncooked vermicelli	1	small onion, chopped
½	cup margarine, melted	1	tablespoon Worcestershire sauce
1	(10¾-ounce) can cream of chicken soup	1	chicken fryer, cooked, boned, and cut into pieces
1	pound Velveeta cheese, cubed		Salt and pepper to taste
1	(10-ounce) can Ro-Tel tomatoes and green chilies		

Cook vermicelli in a covered pot in salted, boiling water for 9 minutes only; then drain. While vermicelli is cooking, mix margarine, soup, and cheese; then add Ro-Tel, onion, Worcestershire sauce, and chicken. Check for salt and pepper. Finally, add the cooked, hot vermicelli, and gently mix to blend well. Check again for salt, then pour into a greased 9×13 inch baking dish. Bake at 350° for 45 minutes or until bubbly. Serves 6 to 8.

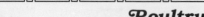
Chicken and Dressing Strata

6 cups corn bread, crumbled	½ cup onions, minced
1 teaspoon celery seed	½ cup margarine, melted
¾ teaspoon salt	1 large fryer, cooked and
½ teaspoon pepper	boned

Sauce:

¼ cup margarine	2 cups chicken broth
1½ teaspoons salt	2 eggs, well beaten
¼ cup flour	1 quart milk

In a large bowl, combine corn bread, celery seed, salt, pepper, onions, and margarine; mix well. Spread in the bottom of a greased 9 × 13 inch pan. Place the boned chicken that has been torn into pieces on top of the corn bread mixture.

Sauce:
In a skillet, melt margarine; add salt and flour. Stir until smooth; then gradually stir in the chicken broth. Cook over medium heat until thickened, stirring constantly. Set aside. Combine beaten eggs and milk. Return skillet to heat and gradually stir in the milk and egg mixture. Cook until mixture is heated and slightly thick. Pour hot sauce evenly over the chicken and corn bread. Bake at 375° for 45 minutes. Serves 6 to 8.

Grand chicken and dressing casserole. When it's cooking, no matter what time of year, the aroma brings visions of Christmas to mind. Casserole can be made a day ahead of time and refrigerated.

German Chicken and Tomatoes

8	slices bacon	¼	teaspoon pepper
6	peeled ripe tomatoes, salted	2	cups milk
1	medium onion, chopped	2	cups cooked chicken,
3	tablespoons plain flour		coarsely diced
1	teaspoon salt		

Fry bacon in skillet until crisp; remove and drain, reserving the bacon drippings. Slice tomatoes thin, and broil or microwave until done. Sauté onion in bacon drippings until lightly browned. Add flour, salt, and pepper to the onion mixture; then slowly stir in the milk. Blend well, and cook until sauce thickens. Add cooked tomatoes to the sauce, and mash tomatoes until they are blended into the sauce. Add chicken; mix well, and heat until bubbling. Serve over Hollard rusk or toast, topped with 2 crossed slices of bacon. Serves 4.

Chicken Enchiladas

1½ cups cooked chicken, cubed		2	(10¾-ounce) cans cream of
1	medium onion, chopped		chicken soup
1	(4-ounce) can diced green	12	frozen corn tortillas, thawed
	chilies	1	pound sharp Cheddar cheese, grated

Mix together chicken, onion, green chilies, and soup. Soak the thawed tortillas in hot water for 3 minutes; drain. In a greased 9×13 inch baking dish, place 6 tortillas. Pour ½ the chicken mixture over the tortillas; sprinkle ½ of the cheese. Repeat layers. Bake at 350° for 30 to 40 minutes.

Nancy Leigh's Chicken Biscuits

3	tablespoons margarine, melted		Salt to taste
3	tablespoons onion, chopped	1	can Hungry Jack biscuits
3	tablespoons celery, chopped	1	(10¾-ounce) can cream of chicken soup
1	drop Tabasco sauce	½	cup milk
¼	teaspoon Worcestershire sauce	¼	cup sour cream
3	chicken breasts, cooked and chopped	1	cup sharp Cheddar cheese, grated

In the melted margarine, sauté onion, celery, Tabasco sauce, and Worcestershire sauce until vegetables are soft; add chicken, and mix together. Salt to taste. With a rolling pin, roll each biscuit flat. Place 1 tablespoon of chicken mixture on each biscuit; roll up and pinch ends together to seal. In a greased, shallow baking dish, arrange the biscuits and bake at 400° for 8-10 minutes. While biscuits are baking, mix the soup, milk, and sour cream. When biscuits are cooked, pour soup mixture over them and top with the cheese. Bake again for 3 to 5 minutes or until cheese is melted.

Whole Smoked Turkey

1   ready-basted 16 pound turkey

Using a covered charcoal grill, build a medium-size fire to one side of the grill. Allow coals to get a grey ashlike covering. Leave coals in a pile; do not spread. Place turkey on the side away from the fire. Cover grill, and leave all vents open. Cook turkey for 3½ hours. Remove from grill, and immediately salt and pepper, fairly heavily, all over the bird. The hot turkey meat will draw in the salt. Carve after the turkey has cooled for 15 minutes. Refrigerate any remaining turkey.

Pork

Pork Roast with Apricot Glaze

1   (12-ounce) can apricot nectar
¼   teaspoon dry mustard
2   teaspoons soy sauce
1   tablespoon sugar
½   teaspoon salt
1   (4-pound) loin pork roast, sliced partially through for easier serving

Preheat oven to 325°. Place apricot nectar in a saucepan, and boil to reduce to ½ volume. Mix mustard, soy sauce, sugar, and salt into the reduced nectar, and remove from heat. Allow the apricot glaze to stand for 2 hours. Place roast in a baking pan, fat side up, with ½ cup water in bottom of the pan. Bake roast 30 to 35 minutes per pound in a preheated oven at 325°. During last 30 minutes of baking time, pour glaze over the roast. Baste roast with the gravy several times during the last 15 minutes of cooking time. Serves 6 to 8.

Pork Chops Potomac

4   lean pork chops
Salt and pepper to taste
2   tablespoons vegetable oil
1   large onion, chopped
½   large green pepper, chopped
3   cups canned tomatoes, mashed
1   cup uncooked regular rice
2   teaspoons salt
1   teaspoon prepared mustard

Salt and pepper pork chops. In a large skillet, heat oil, and brown the chops. Remove chops from skillet, and set aside. Add onion and green pepper to skillet with the drippings, and cook until tender. Stir in the tomatoes, rice, salt, and mustard; mix well. Return pork chops to the skillet. Bring to a boil, cover, and reduce heat to simmer. Cook for 30 to 35 minutes or until rice and chops are tender. Serves 4.

Pork Chops in Mustard Sauce

8 pork chops	2 tablespoons vegetable oil
Prepared mustard	1 (10¾-ounce) can cream of
Plain flour	chicken soup
Salt and pepper	¾ cup water

Spread both sides of pork chops with mustard; then dust with flour, and sprinkle with salt and pepper. In an electric skillet, brown the coated pork chops in the hot oil; remove from skillet. Add soup and water to skillet, and bring to a boil. Return chops, and cover; reduce heat, and simmer for about 35 minutes. Serves 4 to 8.

Indonesian Pork Chops

6 loin pork chops, 1-inch thick	1 medium onion, sliced in
Salt to taste	rings
Pepper to taste	2 tablespoons soy sauce
3 tablespoons vegetable oil	1 teaspoon ground ginger
1 (8-ounce) can Queen Anne	⅛ teaspoon dry mustard
cherries	⅛ teaspoon garlic powder
2 tablespoons brown sugar	1 large green pepper, slivered

Sprinkle chops with salt and pepper on both sides of meat. In an electric skillet, heat oil and brown chops on both sides; then remove from skillet. Drain all except 2 tablespoons of drippings from skillet. Drain the cherries, reserving liquid, and pit the cherries. Mix together cherry liquid, sugar, onions, soy sauce, ginger, mustard, and garlic powder. Return chops to skillet on medium heat. Pour sauce over chops; cover skillet, and simmer for 30 minutes. Add green pepper slivers and cherries; simmer 5 minutes longer. Serve over hot rice. Serves 6.

Chinese Fried Rice

The secret to the success of this dish is using rice that has been dried. Cook rice by the package instructions for the full cooking time then spread in a single layer on a large, shallow pan or on 2 cookie sheets. Bake in the oven at 250° for 20 minutes. Stir rice several times during the baking to dry evenly.

3 cups cooked and dried rice	1 egg
4 slices bacon	1 tablespoon water
1 clove garlic, minced	Salt
2 bunches green onions and tops, chopped	1 tablespoon margarine
	1 to 2 tablespoons soy sauce
2 tablespoons bacon drippings	1 teaspoon MSG

Fry bacon until crisp, and remove to paper towel to drain. Sauté garlic and onion in bacon drippings until transparent, and add bacon that has been crumbled; then set aside. In a small bowl, beat the egg; add water and a sprinkle of salt. Melt margarine, and cook egg, omelet-style; then shred the cooked egg, and add to the onion mixture. Stir cooked rice into onion mixture, and cook over low heat, while tossing, to blend all ingredients. Sprinkle soy sauce and MSG over rice, and mix well. Serves 3 to 4.

A rice lover's delight and a very versatile dish that serves as either a main course or a side dish. Other goodies can be added: diced pork chop; diced ham; small shrimp; well-drained bean sprouts; drained and sliced bamboo shoots. The recipe can be doubled successfully, but make a separate batch if you need to triple.

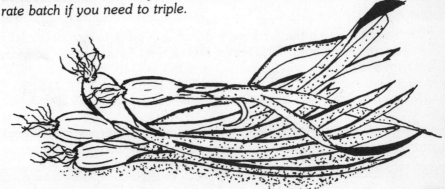

Polynesian Grilled Ham Slices

The ham requires overnight marination.

3	ham slices, ¼-½ inch thick	2	tablespoons cooking sherry
1	(20-ounce) can pineapple slices, liquid reserved	½	teaspoon ground ginger
⅔	cup soy sauce	1	large garlic clove, crushed

Place ham slices in glass baking dishes. Combine pineapple liquid, soy sauce, cooking sherry, ginger, and garlic; mix well. Pour the marinade over the ham slices; then place the pineapple slices on top of the ham. Cover and refrigerate overnight; turn the ham slices once. When ready to cook, discard the marinade, and grill the ham slices over hot coals until ham is thoroughly cooked. Serves 6.

Twice Cured Baked Ham

This is an anticipation-type recipe. By the time the curing process is completed in two weeks, the cooking and serving have become "An Event." Can't tell you how good this is—you just must try it for yourself.

½ ham or large ham roast	Black pepper
Ground cloves	Nutmeg
Brown sugar	Paprika

Remove all fat and skin from the ham. Coat thickly with all the spices, using the paprika as the final layer. Place in a glass baking dish in the refrigerator, uncovered, for at least two weeks. At cooking time, bring to room temperature, and bake in the same dish at 350° for 25 to 30 minutes per pound for a small ham or about 15 minutes per pound for a large ham or until very tender.

*Try to endure the remarks about the strange artifact slinking in the back of the refrigerator. It **does** appear slightly inedible—until serving time.*

European Baked Ham in Pastry

1 (5-7 pound) boneless cooked ham	1 teaspoon salt
1 cup currant jelly	¼ teaspoon dry mustard
3 cups plain flour, sifted	½ cup shortening
2 teaspoons baking powder	¾ cup cold milk

Place ham on a large piece of heavy foil in a baking pan. Spread jelly on top of the ham. Close the foil tightly. Bake at 350° for 10 minutes per pound. (Ham should already be cooked before this cooking time). Sift the flour with baking powder, salt, and dry mustard. Place flour mixture into a food processor and add shortening. Blend to mix; then gradually pour in the cold milk to make a soft dough. Place dough on a floured surface and form into a ball. Roll the dough out to about ¼ inch thickness. When ham is cooked, remove from the oven; reserve ham juices, and allow to cool to the warm stage. While ham is still warm, shape the dough around the ham. Use leftover dough to form designs to decorate the top. Place pastry covered ham in a preheated 450° oven for 10 minutes; reduce heat to 350°, and bake until crust is lightly browned. Serve the reserved juices, with the fat spooned off, in a side bowl.

Stunning entrée, yet very easy to make. The pastry designs can follow your party theme or just be whimsical. Either way it's quite handsome on the table.

Ham on the Pit

1 ham shank or butt	6 ounces prepared mustard
Cola	½ cup brown sugar

In the refrigerator, soak the ham overnight in a bowl of cola, turning several times to marinate all sides. Make a paste of the mustard and brown sugar; then coat the ham with the paste. Cook over indirect coals on a covered grill, until ham is thoroughly done, and tender.

Ham Heidelberg

½ ham, 6-8 pounds
8 ounces currant jelly
½ cup bourbon or sherry

1 teaspoon dry mustard
2 tablespoons brown sugar

Trim ham of almost all excess fat. Combine currant jelly, bourbon, dry mustard, and brown sugar. Using the handle of a wooden spoon, punch deep holes all over the ham. Press the jelly mixture into the holes, holding the hole open with the spoon handle. Coat the ham with the unused portion of the jelly mixture. Bake ham, covered, at 350° for 25 minutes per pound. Remove cover for the final 20 minutes of baking time.

To bone the ham for easy carving, allow ham to cool just enough to touch. With a small sharp knife, cut around all bones. Ham will have to be split in 1 or 2 places to remove the bones. When all bone is removed, press any pieces that are loose back into place, and re-form ham into the original shape. Wrap very tightly in aluminum foil, and refrigerate until cold. Amazing! The ham "glues" itself back together, and you don't have to wrestle the bone to slice.

Vermicelli Carbonara

1 cup uncooked ham, cubed
⅓ cup green pepper, minced
½ cup onion, sliced
½ cup mushrooms, sliced
1 egg, well beaten

1 (8-ounce) package vermicelli
¼ cup margarine
½ cup Half and Half
Salt and pepper to taste
½ cup Parmesan cheese, grated

Cube ham, chop vegetables, beat egg, and have other ingredients measured and ready for use. In a large pot, cook vermicelli in boiling salted water for exactly 9 minutes. Immediately remove from heat and drain. While the vermicelli is cooking, melt margarine, and sauté ham, onion, green pepper, and mushrooms until tender, and ham is done. Keeping the ham mixture hot, add the hot, drained vermicelli, and toss carefully to avoid breaking the vermicelli. Pour egg into Half and Half, and beat; then pour it over the vermicelli, and toss carefully again. Taste for salt and pepper; then sprinkle with Parmesan cheese. Stir, mixing cheese and heating at the same time; serve hot. Serves 4.

Joan's Heavenly Ham Casserole

3   medium cooked potatoes,
    peeled and sliced
1   (10-ounce) package frozen
    broccoli spears
¼   cup margarine
½   teaspoon salt
2   tablespoons plain flour

1   cup milk
1   cup sharp Cheddar cheese,
    grated
1   ham steak, ½ to 1-inch thick
Extra salt and pepper
Paprika

Cook potatoes; then cook broccoli by directions on the package until just tender; drain. In a skillet, melt margarine; add salt and flour, and stir until smooth. Gradually add milk, keeping mixture smooth, and cook until thickened, stirring constantly. Then add cheese, and stir until melted. Cut ham steak into four pieces, and place in a greased baking dish. Make layers, beginning with potatoes, a little extra salt and pepper on them, and broccoli spears. Pour sauce over all ingredients, and sprinkle with paprika. Bake at 350° for 45 minutes. Serves 3 to 4.

The ham juice soaking into the potatoes really gives this dish a marvelous flavor. It even appeals to "non-broccoli lovers." Add the color to the flavor, and it's hard to top.

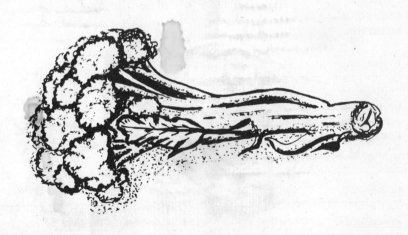

Seafood

Shrimp Neptune

6   ounces green noodles
    (spinach)
2   pounds shrimp, peeled
½   cup margarine
1   (10¾-ounce) can cream of
    mushroom soup
1   cup sour cream

1   cup mayonnaise
½   teaspoon Dijon mustard
1   tablespoon chives, chopped
3   teaspoons cooking sherry
1   cup sharp Cheddar cheese,
    grated

Cook green noodles according to package directions, and drain. In a skillet, sauté raw shrimp in the margarine 5 minutes or until pink. Combine cream of mushroom soup, sour cream, mayonnaise, mustard, chives, and sherry; mix until well blended. In a greased 9 × 13 inch baking dish, make layers beginning with the green noodles, shrimp, and sauce; then top with the cheese. Bake at 350° for 35 minutes. Serves 8 to 10.

Shrimp lovers, this one is "a must." Indescribably delicious. Neptune would find it befitting of his world.

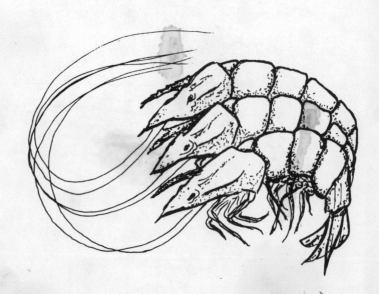

Cajun Barbecued Shrimp

1 cup margarine	1 cup vegetable oil
½ teaspoon oregano	4 bay leaves
2 large cloves garlic, crushed	1 teaspoon salt or more
½ teaspoon basil	¼ teaspoon rosemary
½ teaspoon cayenne pepper	2 tablespoons lemon juice
½ teaspoon black pepper	1 tablespoon paprika
3 pounds large raw shrimp, unpeeled	1 loaf fresh French bread, uncut

In a Dutch oven, add all ingredients except shrimp. Bring to a boil, stirring constantly; then reduce heat to simmer, and cook for 10 minutes. Remove from heat, and let sauce cool completely. Leaving shells on the shrimp, wash them very thoroughly in several changes of running water; drain. After sauce has cooled, return sauce to heat, and bring to a boil. Add shrimp, and cook until mixture comes back to a boil. Cook until shrimp turn pink. Pour shrimp and sauce into a casserole, and bake at 425° for 15 minutes. Serve in large soup bowls with fresh, hot French bread for dipping into the sauce. Serves 4.

The French bread should be served hot and uncut, so that a piece has to be torn off the loaf. Dipping the bread into the sauce is the proper way to eat this Cajun dish. It's messy, but delicious. Have plenty of napkins and lobster bibs for your guests.

Marinated Fried Shrimp

Marinate shrimp overnight.

1½-2 pounds raw shrimp,
   medium to large size
Juice of 1 large lemon
1   tablespoon Worcestershire
   sauce
1   tablespoon salt
2   cups water

Plain flour
2   eggs, well beaten (more if
   needed)
Ritz cracker crumbs
Vegetable oil for frying
Salt, if needed

Peel raw shrimp, and place into a large glass container or jar with a cover. Add lemon juice, Worcestershire sauce, salt, and water. Cover container, and shake very well to mix ingredients and shrimp. Refrigerate overnight. Shake several times during the marinating process. Before frying, drain shrimp, and coat with flour. Dip coated shrimp into the beaten eggs; then roll in cracker crumbs to completely coat. Deep fry to a golden brown. Do not overcook; shrimp cook quickly. Drain on paper towels. Lightly salt, if needed. Keep warm on a warming tray uncovered.

These shrimp are superb! The marinade is very light and delicate, enhancing the shrimp flavor. Serve plenty to the seafood lovers. If time is a problem, begin 2 days in advance of serving. Marinate the first day; then batter the second day. Place battered, uncooked shrimp on a cookie sheet, cover with plastic wrap, and freeze. Thaw and fry on serving day.

Mike's Grilled Gulf Shrimp

2 pounds large raw shrimp, unpeeled
1 cup margarine, melted
½ cup lemon juice

Garlic salt to taste
Coarse ground black pepper to taste

Wash unpeeled shrimp in 6 changes of fresh water. Partially peel shrimp, leaving the tail section of the peel in place. Rinse shrimp in running water; drain thoroughly. In a large bowl, combine melted margarine, lemon juice, garlic salt, and pepper; mix well. Place drained shrimp in the marinade for about 2 hours; refrigerate. Stir occasionally to marinate all the shrimp. Thread shrimp onto skewers, and grill over hot coals until shrimp turn pink; turn skewers, and grill on reverse side until pink. Allow shrimp to remain on the grill 5 minutes longer. Do not overcook; shrimp cook quickly. Serves 4.

For the real shrimp lover, this is a fantastic way to enjoy it. Eating the grilled shrimp, you can almost hear the lapping of the surf and smell the salty air of those beautiful Gulf beaches. After such a flowery description, I can't decide if I want to eat shrimp or head for the beach!

Shrimp New Orleans

2   pounds raw shrimp,
    unpeeled
1   pound butter
Black pepper to taste

Garlic salt to taste
Lemon juice to taste
2   teaspoons crab boil
Fresh French bread

Several hours before preparing the dish for serving, wash the shrimp in 6 changes of fresh water. Allow the shrimp to completely drain in a colander in the refrigerator until cooking time. At cooking time, combine in a saucepan the butter, lots of black pepper, garlic salt, lemon juice, and the crab boil; set aside. Place the unpeeled shrimp in a flat 3-quart baking dish. Bring the butter sauce to a boil, and pour over the shrimp. Immediately, put the shrimp under a hot broiler. Allow shrimp to turn pink on one side; then turn shrimp over to broil until pink on the other side. Turn oven off, and allow shrimp to remain in hot oven 5 minutes longer. Serve hot in bowls with hot French bread. Serves 3 to 4.

To eat this dish properly, you'll need a lobster bib, plenty of napkins, and dinner partners that are connoisseurs of the New Orleans style of "sopping" the shrimp sauce with French bread. Magnifique!

Shrimp a la Capri

4 ounces raw vermicelli, broken in half	3 tablespoons Parmesan cheese, grated
½ cup margarine	½ teaspoon salt
1 small clove garlic, minced	¼ teaspoon coarse ground pepper
8 large raw shrimp, peeled and diced	½ teaspoon MSG
4 large mushrooms, sliced	Extra grated Parmesan cheese to sprinkle

Cook vermicelli in a covered pot in salted boiling water for exactly 9 minutes. Rinse in cold water and drain; then set aside. In a large non-stick skillet, heat margarine and sauté garlic, shrimp, and mushrooms for 5 minutes or until shrimp are pink. Add vermicelli and stir carefully to coat with margarine mixture. Continue to heat slowly, and add Parmesan cheese, salt, pepper, and MSG. Gently toss and turn until all ingredients are mixed and very hot. Serve immediately with the extra Parmesan cheese sprinkled on top. Serves 2.

The aroma brings to mind romantic Italy, by the sea, with a faint whiff of garlic and fresh shrimp. I think you'll have to have a little Soave to go with this one. Mmmmm . . .

Shrimp Creole

1	medium onion, chopped	⅛	teaspoon garlic salt
1	medium green pepper, chopped	2	drops Tabasco sauce
2	tablespoons margarine	½	teaspoon Worcestershire sauce
1	(16-ounce) can tomatoes, chopped and mashed	1	cup water
¼	teaspoon salt	1	pound raw shrimp, peeled
1	small clove garlic, minced		Hot rice

In a large skillet, sauté onion and green pepper in the margarine until limp. Add tomatoes, salt, garlic, garlic salt, Tabasco sauce, and Worcestershire sauce. Cook on medium heat for 10 minutes. Add water, stir, and cook for another 5 minutes. Add shrimp and cook, stirring, until the shrimp turn pink. Cook 3 minutes longer. Remove from heat. Serve over hot rice. Serves 2 to 4.

Quick, Great Cocktail Sauce

4	tablespoons horseradish	1	cup catsup
2	drops Tabasco sauce	3	tablespoons lemon juice

Mix all ingredients. Sauce can be stored in the refrigerator in a tightly covered jar to use when needed. Yield: 1 cup.

Tartar Sauce for Seafood

1	tablespoon onion, grated	¼	cup parsley, chopped
1	whole dill pickle, diced	1	cup mayonnaise
1	tablespoon lemon juice	1	tablespoon capers, minced

Mix all ingredients until well blended. Refrigerate. Yield: 1½ cups.

Maryland Crab Cakes

2 tablespoons mayonnaise	½ teaspoon cayenne pepper
1 egg, beaten	1 drop Tabasco sauce
½ teaspoon dry mustard	1 pound lump crabmeat
½ teaspoon salt	2 tablespoons fine cracker
½ small onion, minced	crumbs

Combine mayonnaise, egg, mustard, salt, onion, cayenne, and Tabasco sauce; mix well. Carefully stir in the crabmeat and cracker crumbs, taking care not to break up the crabmeat lumps. Shape into dinner-size cakes. Fry in vegetable oil until browned on both sides. Serves 4.

Fresh Whole Salmon

Salt and pepper	1-2 cloves garlic, completely
Whole salmon split into 2 fillets	crushed
Margarine, softened	Lemon juice
	Mayonnaise

Salt and pepper both sides of the fillets. Make a generous paste (for the size of the fillets) of softened margarine, crushed garlic, and a generous amount of lemon juice. The lemon juice and margarine do not mix very well, but the overall effect will be successful. Spread paste over the flesh side of the fillets to completely cover the flesh. Spread mayonnaise completely over the skin side of the fillets. Make a "tent" of aluminum foil to lightly stand over fillets while they cook; then place fillets on the grill (skin and mayonnaise side down) over **indirect** heat with the "tents" in place. Cover grill, leave all vents open, and let salmon cook for about 20-30 minutes; do not turn fillets over. Check salmon for doneness, do not overcook. The salmon should be flaky when tested with a fork.

Marvelous Crab Crêpes

Crêpes:

1 cup cold water	2 cups plain flour
1 cup cold milk	4 tablespoons margarine,
4 eggs	melted
½ teaspoon salt	

Filling:

4 tablespoons green onion, chopped	1 tablespoon cooking sherry
	1 pound fresh crabmeat
4 tablespoons margarine	Salt and pepper

Sauce:

4 tablespoons margarine	2 egg yolks
5 tablespoons plain flour	½ cup heavy cream
2 cups milk	¾ cup Swiss cheese, grated
Salt and pepper	

Directions for crêpes:
Place all ingredients into a food processor with steel blade or a blender. Blend until smooth. Refrigerate batter for at least 2 hours. Using a 6-inch crêpe pan or non-stick skillet, heat a few drops of vegetable oil. Pour just enough batter into pan to cover the bottom. Cook over medium heat until crêpe is very light brown. Turn crêpe, and cook other side. Continue making crêpes until all batter is used.

Filling instructions:
Sauté onion in the margarine. Add sherry; then carefully stir in crabmeat. Salt and pepper to taste. Set aside.

Sauce instructions:
In a skillet, melt margarine, and stir in flour until smooth. Stirring constantly, gradually add milk, keeping the sauce smooth. Cook over medium heat, while stirring, until thickened. Salt and pepper to taste, and allow to cool slightly. Beat egg yolks and cream. Add the yolks and cream to the sauce while beating. Return to heat and cook, while stirring, until thickened. Add cheese and blend. Pour sauce into filling mixture; mix well. Allow mixture to cool before assembling the crêpes.

To assemble:
Reserve some crabmeat mixture (about 1½ cups), to pour over filled crêpes. Fill each crêpe with crabmeat mixture, and roll or form a package by folding the ends. Place seam side down in a greased casserole. Pour reserved crabmeat mixture over rolled crêpes. Bake at 325° until the crêpes are hot and sauce is bubbling. Yield: about 25 to 29 crêpes.

Crab Dartmouth

4   saltine crackers, rolled very
    fine
6   tablespoons margarine
½   cup milk
2   eggs
1   tablespoon mayonnaise

1   tablespoon Worcestershire
    sauce
1   teaspoon prepared mustard
½   teaspoon salt
Pepper to taste
1   tablespoon chopped parsley
1   pound crabmeat

In a saucepan, combine cracker crumbs, margarine, and milk. Heat on low until the margarine is melted. Remove from heat, and allow to cool. Beat eggs well, and add to the cooled milk mixture. Stir in the mayonnaise, Worcestershire sauce, mustard, salt, pepper, and parsley; mix well. Carefully stir in the crabmeat; do not break the lumps of crab. Pour into a greased shallow casserole. Bake at 350° for 35-45 minutes or until browned and set. Serves 4 to 6.

Crabmeat Imperial

⅓   green pepper, minced
¾   pimento, minced
1   teaspoon English mustard
½   teaspoon salt
⅛   teaspoon white pepper

1   egg
⅓   cup mayonnaise
1   pound lump crabmeat
Additional mayonnaise
Paprika

Mix green pepper and pimento; add mustard, salt, white pepper, egg, and mayonnaise; mix well. Add crabmeat, and mix very carefully, not breaking the lumps. Divide mixture into 4 crab shells or individual casseroles. Top with a small coating of mayonnaise; then sprinkle with paprika. Bake at 350° for 15 minutes. Serves 4.

Crisp Fried Oysters

Medium oysters
Self-rising corn meal

Vegetable oil
Salt and pepper

Drain oysters; then place one at a time into a plastic bag with the corn meal. Shake bag to coat each oyster. Place the coated oysters on a cookie sheet, and freeze for 20-30 minutes. Fry oysters, unthawed, in hot to medium oil until brown and crisp. Drain well on paper towels, and salt to taste. Keep oysters warm, uncovered, on a warming tray.

Pit Steamed Oysters

Using a covered charcoal or gas grill, build a fire to white hot coals; then scatter the coals. Place as many unopened oysters on the grill rack as it will hold. Cover the shells with a large wet burlap sack. Close top of grill, and let oysters cook until the shells can be heard popping open. Remove the oyster shells with an oven mitt, and finish opening with an oyster knife. Dip hot oysters in sauces.

Cocktail Sauce:

2   cups catsup
2   tablespoons prepared
    horseradish

2   tablespoons lemon juice
1   teaspoon Worcestershire
    sauce

Mix well, and refrigerate to keep.

Lemon Butter Sauce:

1   cup butter
4   tablespoons lemon juice

1   clove garlic, crushed

Mix well, and keep this hot on the side of the grill.

This process is very slow, so have a few good friends, hors d'oeuvres, raw oysters, and fried oysters, etc., to serve with these steamed oysters.

Eggs and Cheese

Almond-Topped Crab Quiche

1 (9-inch) deep-dish pie shell, unbaked
1 cup Swiss cheese, grated
½ pound fresh crabmeat
2 green onions, sliced
3 eggs
1 cup Half and Half
½ teaspoon salt
½ teaspoon lemon rind, grated
Dash of dry mustard
Dash of black pepper
¼ cup sliced almonds

In a 400° preheated oven, bake the pie shell for 3 minutes; then remove from oven, and gently prick pie shell with a fork. Bake 5 minutes longer, and let cool. Sprinkle cheese in the cooled shell evenly; then place crabmeat on top of cheese, followed by the green onion. Beat eggs until foamy; stir in Half and Half, salt, lemon rind, dry mustard, and pepper. Pour the egg mixture into the pie shell, and sprinkle with almonds. Bake at 325° for 1 hour or until set. Let the quiche stand for 10 minutes before serving.

Edna's Blintzes

Batter:

4 **eggs**	1 **cup milk**
1 **cup plain flour**	1 **teaspoon salt**

Filling:

1½ **pounds cottage cheese, drained**	2 **egg yolks, beaten**
	1 **teaspoon sugar**

Batter:
Mix all batter ingredients in a food processor or blender until well-blended. Heat a 6-inch non-stick skillet; add a few drops of vegetable oil, and coat skillet. Pour off any excess oil. Return skillet to medium heat; pour 2 to 3 tablespoons batter into skillet, and tilt skillet to coat the bottom of skillet with batter. Cook, not browning, until sides begin to curl and batter is cooked. Remove crêpe to a plate (only cook one side). Repeat until all batter is used.

Filling:
After draining cottage cheese, press cottage cheese with a fork to break curds and drain again. Mix well-drained cottage cheese with egg yolks and sugar. Place a heaping tablespoon of filling into the center of the crêpe; then fold on three sides and tuck the fourth side in, envelope-style. Refrigerate or freeze. Just before serving, slowly pan fry blintzes in 2 tablespoons margarine until very light brown. Serve hot with strawberry preserves, sour cream, fresh fruit, and cinnamon sugar as topping selections. Yield: 13 or 14.

Blintzes Soufflé

½ cup margarine, melted
1 recipe of Edna's Blintzes
4 eggs, well beaten

1½ cups sour cream
2 tablespoons sugar
½ teaspoon vanilla

Pour melted margarine into a flat 2-quart baking dish. Place blintzes in the baking dish in a single layer. Mix together the beaten eggs, sour cream, sugar, and vanilla until well blended. Pour over the blintzes. Bake at 350° for 45 minutes or until top of soufflé starts to brown. Serve hot with strawberry preserves, fresh slices of strawberries, sour cream, or cinnamon sugar as topping selections. Serves 6 or 7.

Baddeck Scotch Eggs

3 hard-boiled eggs, cooled
½ pound sausage, softened
1 egg, well beaten

Bread crumbs
Butter slices

Preheat deep fat to 375°. Shell the hard-boiled eggs, and completely surround the eggs with the softened sausage meat. Dip them into the beaten egg, and roll in bread crumbs. Fry 3-4 minutes, or until golden brown, and sausage is done. Cut eggs in half, and place a slice of butter in the center.

Baddeck is any sailor's dream, with lots of coves to explore and possibly a charming Bed and Breakfast for overnight. There you might be served these Scotch Eggs by some of the many descendants of Scotland who live on Cape Breton Island at Nova Scotia's northernmost tip. Baddeck was once the home of one of the world's greatest inventors, Alexander Graham Bell. A visit there will certainly enhance the flavor of these delicious eggs.

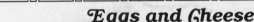

Baked Cheese Grits

1 cup grits	Milk
½ cup margarine	Garlic salt to taste
12 ounces sharp Cheddar cheese	3 eggs, well beaten
	2 drops Tabasco sauce

Cook grits according to package directions. When grits are cooked, add margarine, cheese, and enough milk to make grits slightly "soupy." Heat on low to allow cheese to melt; stir to blend. Add garlic salt to taste. Stir in eggs and Tabasco sauce; mix well. Pour into a greased casserole. Bake at 350° for 50 to 60 minutes. Remove from oven, and allow casserole to cool for about 5 minutes before serving. Serves 6 to 8.

Very Southern casserole that's great for breakfast, brunch, or Sunday night light supper since it can be made ahead and refrigerated or frozen. Decorate the top with strips of cut American cheese to suit the occasion. Seems that Scrooge was decorating last Christmas morning's casserole, since the message read "Bah Humbug!" Was great for a sleepy morning laugh, but definitely did not set the mood for such a special day.

Creamed Eggs on Toast

6 hard boiled eggs	Salt and pepper to taste
4 tablespoons margarine	4 slices crisp toast
4 tablespoons plain flour	Paprika
2 cups milk	

Peel the hard boiled eggs, and set aside. In a skillet, melt the margarine, and stir in flour until smooth. Stirring constantly, gradually add milk, keeping the sauce smooth. Cook over medium heat, while stirring, until thickened; add salt and pepper to taste. Chop peeled eggs, and gently stir into the cream sauce. Test again for salt. Serve hot over the toast; garnish with paprika. Serves 4.

Breakfast Sausage Casserole

Make at least one day before serving.

1	pound medium or hot sausage	8	eggs, well beaten
1	large onion, chopped	4	cups milk
12	slices white bread, cut in quarters	1½	teaspoons salt
10	ounces sharp Cheddar cheese, grated	¼	teaspoon pepper
		½	teaspoon dry mustard

Cook sausage until browned; drain all drippings except 2 tablespoons. Sauté the onion in the reserved drippings until tender. In a greased 9 × 13 inch baking dish, layer the ingredients. Begin with ½ of the bread, then ½ sausage, ½ onions, and ½ cheese; repeat layers. Beat together the eggs, milk, salt, pepper, and dry mustard; then pour over the layers. Cover and refrigerate for at least overnight before cooking. When ready to bake, remove baking dish from refrigerator 1 hour before baking to bring to room temperature; then bake at 350° for 50 minutes. Serves 10 to 12.

Green Chilies and Cheese Casserole

1	egg, well beaten	1	(4-ounce) can diced green chilies
1	cup milk	8	ounces sharp Cheddar cheese, grated
⅓	cup Bisquick		

In an electric mixer, beat egg and milk on medium speed; add Bisquick, and blend well. By hand, stir in chilies and cheese; mix well. Pour into a greased 1½-quart casserole. Bake at 350° for 30 to 45 minutes or until well set.

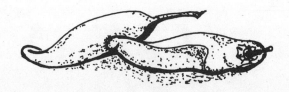

Cheese and Sausage Breakfast Wheel

2   packages Pillsbury
    refrigerated crescent rolls
1   pound bulk pork sausage,
    medium hot
16 ounces frozen hash browns

1½ cups sharp Cheddar cheese,
    grated
½   teaspoon salt
4   eggs, well beaten
¼   cup Parmesan cheese, grated

Preheat oven to 375°. Separate crescent rolls into triangles, and place touching on a greased pizza pan with pointed ends toward the center. Press the roll seams together to form a crust. Cook sausage and crumble; drain. Sprinkle the sausage over the crust evenly. Sprinkle frozen hash browns over sausage. Cover the hash browns with the Cheddar cheese. Add salt to beaten eggs, and pour over all layers. Top with the Parmesan cheese. Bake in a preheated oven at 375° for 20 to 25 minutes. Cut like pizza to serve. Serves 6 to 8.

Crabmeat Omelet

4   tablespoons margarine,
    divided
1   rib celery, minced
1   small onion, minced

4   eggs
1   pound lump crabmeat
Salt and pepper to taste

In a non-stick skillet, melt 2 tablespoons of the margarine; sauté the celery and onion until tender. Remove onion mixture from the skillet, and wipe clean. Melt remaining 2 tablespoons of margarine in the skillet on medium heat. Beat the eggs well; add crabmeat, salt, and pepper. Stir in the onion mixture, and blend well. Pour egg mixture into skillet. Cook on medium heat until the eggs are almost completely set. Run spatula under one side of omelet, and flip on top of other side, to form a semi-circle. Cook a few minutes longer to allow egg to completely set. Do not brown the omelet. Serves 4.

Huevos Rancheros

1½ pounds ground beef, browned, drained, and crumbled
1 teaspoon cumin powder
1 teaspoon pepper
Garlic salt to taste
1 (15-ounce) can refried beans
4 tablespoons mild taco sauce
4 tablespoons hot taco sauce
1 tablespoon Worcestershire sauce
6 drops Tabasco sauce
4 corn tortillas
4 eggs
4 tablespoons sour cream, if desired
½ cup mild onion, minced
2 cups sharp Cheddar cheese, grated
Taco sauce for topping

Combine cooked ground beef with cumin, pepper, and garlic salt. Add beans, both taco sauces, Worcestershire sauce, and Tabasco sauce; mix well. Pour into a greased casserole, and bake the mixture in the oven on 325° for ½ hour. Add more taco sauce if mixture needs more moisture. Fry tortillas in hot oil until crisp. Drain, and keep warm; do not cover. Fry eggs, over light. Top each tortilla with meat sauce, sour cream, minced onion, fried egg, and ¼ of the cheese. Serve taco sauce on the side in a bowl. Serves 4.

Superb flavors of old Mexico. The eggs can also be poached, but do not leave them off. They add to the flavor authenticity.

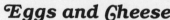

Creole Eggs

12 tablespoons margarine, divided
7 tablespoons plain flour, divided
2 cups milk
Salt and pepper to taste
3 small onions, minced
1 medium green pepper, minced
1 (16-ounce) can tomatoes, chopped
2 tablespoons Worcestershire sauce
Cayenne pepper to taste
14 hard boiled eggs, peeled and chopped
Corn flakes, crushed

In a skillet, melt 4 tablespoons of the margarine; stir in 5 tablespoons of the flour until smooth. Gradually add milk, keeping the mixture smooth; stir constantly, while cooking, over medium heat until sauce thickens. Add salt and pepper to taste. In another skillet, melt the remaining 8 tablespoons margarine, and sauté onions and green pepper until tender. Stir in remaining 2 tablespoons flour, tomatoes, Worcestershire, and cayenne pepper. Cook and blend for 1 minute. Make layers of the ingredients in a greased 9×13 inch baking dish. Begin with a layer of chopped egg, then a layer of sauce, and repeat. Just before serving, add a heavy layer of the crushed corn flakes. Bake at 350° for 25 to 30 minutes or until bubbly. Serves 8 to 12.

If this dish is assembled ahead of time and refrigerated, blot up or spoon off any extra watery accumulation before adding the corn flake crumbs.

Game, Lamb, Veal

Smothered Doves or Quail

12 birds
Salt and pepper
Plain flour

6-8 tablespoons margarine
2   cups water
2   teaspoons Worcestershire

Salt and pepper the birds on all surfaces. Sift flour over the birds to lightly coat the whole bird. Place the birds in a casserole, and dot birds with the margarine. Combine water and Worcestershire sauce; then pour the water mixture into the pan. Cover casserole, and bake at 350° for at least 1 hour or until tender. Baste the birds several times during cooking time. Serves 4.

Long ago were the days when my grandfather and his entourage of friends, bird dogs, and helpers would set out hours before daylight for his bird-hunting property in South Alabama. My grandmother would have invited friends for a "bird supper." Granddaddy would check the guest list before leaving to make certain that he brought home enough birds for the dinner party, plus enough for all in his hunting party.

Barbecued Leg of Lamb, Holly Hill Style

5-6 pound fresh leg of lamb (have butcher remove gland from leg of lamb)	Salt

Sauce:

24	ounces catsup	Salt, if desired	
4	tablespoons Worcestershire sauce	4	cups water
		4	tablespoons vinegar
Juice of 2 lemons		4	slices of lemon
½	teaspoon dry mustard	¼	teaspoon pepper

Preheat oven to 500°. With a sharp knife, remove all fat and skin from lamb; then score the lamb, and salt. In a saucepan, combine all sauce ingredients, and bring to a boil; reduce heat, and simmer until slightly thickened. Place lamb in a large roaster pan that has a lid, and add about ½ inch of water in bottom of pan. Roast lamb, uncovered, at 500° for 15 minutes; reduce heat to 425°, and roast for 15 minutes more. Pour sauce over lamb, cover and reduce heat to 325°. Cook, basting often, for about 2 hours or until very tender. Serve lamb sliced hot with rice and lamb gravy.

Veal Picatta

2	pounds veal, sliced and pounded very thin	1	clove garlic, crushed
		1½	lemons, divided
Salt and pepper to taste		2	tablespoons parsley, chopped and divided
2	tablespoons vegetable oil		
3	tablespoons margarine		

Sprinkle both sides of veal with salt and pepper; then cut into 2-inch-wide strips. Brown the veal in hot oil in a skillet until done; drain and set aside. In a small saucepan, melt margarine until bubbling; then add garlic, juice of the ½ lemon, and 1 tablespoon of the parsley. Heat until bubbling again, and add veal just long enough to heat veal. Serve garnished with the whole lemon sliced very thin on top of veal strips and the remaining parsley sprinkled over all. Serves 4.

Vegetables

My Mother's Asparagus Casserole

3 tablespoons margarine
2½ tablespoons plain flour
2 cups milk
3 cups sharp Cheddar cheese, grated and divided

4 (15-ounce) cans Green Giant extra long spears of asparagus, drained
¾ cup pecans or almonds, chopped

In a skillet, melt margarine, and stir in flour until smooth. Stirring constantly, gradually add milk, keeping the sauce smooth. Cook over medium heat while stirring until thickened. Add 2 cups of the grated cheese, and stir while cooking, over low heat until cheese is melted. In a greased casserole, carefully place the asparagus spears; then cover with the cheese sauce. Sprinkle the chopped nuts evenly over the sauce; top with the remaining 1 cup of grated cheese. Bake at 350° until casserole is very hot and bubbling.

My mother has had this wonderful dish on her traditional Thanksgiving menu since before I was around to enjoy it! It's great for dinner anytime and especially for dinner parties.

Crisp Topped Asparagus Casserole

2 (15-ounce) cans Green Giant extra long spears of asparagus, liquid reserved
½ cup margarine
4 tablespoons plain flour
Salt and pepper

Ritz cracker crumbs
2 hard-boiled eggs, peeled and sliced
Extra margarine to dot top of casserole

Drain asparagus and reserve the liquid. In a skillet, melt margarine, and stir in flour until smooth. Stirring constantly, gradually add asparagus liquid, keeping the sauce smooth. Cook over medium heat, while stirring, until thickened; add salt and pepper to taste. In a greased casserole, sprinkle a layer of cracker crumbs; cover with ½ of the sauce. Carefully place all of the asparagus spears in the layer of sauce. Place all of the egg slices over asparagus, and top with the remaining sauce. Sprinkle with remaining cracker crumbs, and dot with margarine. Bake at 350° for 35 minutes or until bubbling. Serves 6.

Green Beans Williamsburg

2 (9-ounce) packages frozen
   French-style green beans
½ cup onion, chopped
7 slices raw bacon, diced
¼ cup plain flour
1½ cups water

2 teaspoons dry chicken
   bouillon
⅛ teaspoon pepper
½ cup sharp Cheddar cheese,
   grated

Prepare green beans as directed on the package; drain and set aside. In a skillet, sauté onions as bacon is frying, stirring occasionally. When bacon is cooked, blend flour into onion mixture; then gradually stir in water, bouillon, and pepper. Cook over medium heat, stirring, until sauce is thick. Gently add the drained green beans, and mix well. Pour into a greased 1½-quart casserole, and sprinkle with the cheese. Bake at 350° for 30 minutes or until bubbly. Serves 8.

Swiss Green Beans

2 teaspoons margarine
2 teaspoons plain flour
1 teaspoon salt
¼ teaspoon pepper
½ teaspoon sugar
½ small onion, grated

8 ounces sour cream
10 ounces Swiss cheese, grated
2 (16-ounce) cans whole green
   beans, drained
Buttered cracker crumbs

In a non-stick skillet, melt the margarine; then stir in flour, salt, pepper, sugar, and onion. Heat on low and add sour cream, stirring until thickened. Add cheese and stir until melted. Pour the drained green beans into sauce and gently mix to coat the beans. Put mixture into a greased, flat casserole; top with buttered bread crumbs. Bake at 400° for 20 to 25 minutes. Serves 8.

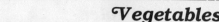
My Mother's Butter Beans

2-3 cups fresh shelled butter
    beans or 2 (10-ounce)
    packages frozen petite lima
    beans
Salt

4   tablespoons margarine
Black pepper
1   tablespoon plain flour
Water

Cook the butter beans in boiling, salted water until tender, taking care
that they do not overcook and get mushy. Add margarine to the liquid
in the saucepan, and be generous with the pepper. In a small cup, add
the flour and just enough water to stir into a smooth paste. Stir flour
mixture into the butter bean liquid; mix well. Heat and stir to slightly
thicken; serve hot. Serves 4-6.

*My mother's touch of thickening the butter bean liquid, plus the black
pepper, adds that "something extra."*

Barbecued Baked Beans

1   (31-ounce) can pork and
    beans
¼ cup light corn syrup
¼ cup catsup
1 large onion, chopped

2   tablespoons prepared
    mustard
½ tablespoon chili powder
1   tablespoon vinegar
Salt to taste
6   slices raw bacon

Combine all ingredients except the bacon. Pour into a greased casserole; place the raw bacon slices on top. Cover, and bake at 300° for 2
hours. Serves 6.

Baked Broccoli Casserole

2 (10-ounce) packages chopped broccoli
1 scant cup mayonnaise
1 tablespoon lemon juice
2 eggs, well beaten

1 cup sharp Cheddar cheese, grated
1 (10¾-ounce) can cream of mushroom soup
½ medium onion, chopped
Salt and pepper to taste

Preheat oven to 350°. Thaw the broccoli, then mix in all other ingredients until well blended. Pour into a greased casserole, and bake at 350° for 50-55 minutes. Serves 6.

Broccoli and Rice Casserole

3 (10-ounce) packages frozen chopped broccoli
¼ cup margarine
1 large onion, chopped
1 to 1½ cups cooked rice

1 (10¾-ounce) can cream of chicken soup
1 (8-ounce) jar Cheez Whiz
Paprika

Cook broccoli as directed on package; drain. Melt margarine, and sauté onion until tender. Add rice, soup, and cheese to the onion. Stir in the drained broccoli, and blend all ingredients. Pour into a greased casserole, and sprinkle top with paprika. Bake at 350° for 20 minutes or until bubbling. Serves 6-8.

Broccoli and Tomato Parmesan

2 (10-ounce) packages frozen
   chopped broccoli
8 ounces sliced mushrooms,
   drained
2 tablespoons margarine,
   melted
1 cup sour cream

Dash Tabasco sauce
Salt and pepper to taste
1 egg, beaten
3-4 fresh tomatoes, peeled and
   sliced
¾ cup grated Parmesan cheese,
   divided

Preheat oven to 400°. Cook broccoli according to package directions; drain. Sauté drained mushrooms in the margarine for 2-3 minutes. Remove from heat, and stir in the sour cream and drained broccoli. Add Tabasco sauce, salt, and pepper to taste. Mix in the beaten egg until well-blended. Place the broccoli mixture into a greased 2-quart baking dish. Sprinkle the tomatoes with salt, pepper, and some of the Parmesan cheese on both sides; then place on top of the broccoli layer. Sprinkle the remaining Parmesan cheese on top of the casserole. Bake in a preheated oven at 400° for 40 minutes or until top is browned. Serves 8.

Cheesy Cabbage Casserole

1 medium head cabbage,
   shredded
5 tablespoons margarine,
   melted and divided
3 tablespoons plain flour
1 teaspoon salt

Dash of red pepper (optional)
1½ cups milk
1 cup sharp Cheddar cheese,
   grated
1 cup bread crumbs

In a saucepan, cook cabbage in boiling, salted water for 8 minutes. Drain the cabbage. In a skillet, melt 3 tablespoons of the margarine; add flour, salt and red pepper, stirring until smooth. Then slowly add milk, keeping the sauce smooth; cook until thickened, stirring constantly. Add cheese to the hot sauce; blend. Mix bread crumbs with the remaining 2 tablespoons margarine. In a greased casserole, layer the cabbage, the sauce, and the crumbs; repeat layers. Bake at 350° for 30 minutes. Serves 4-6.

Stir-fried Cabbage

2   slices bacon
1   large onion, sliced in thin
    rings
¼   large cabbage, thinly
    shredded

Dash cayenne pepper
½   teaspoon ground ginger
1   tablespoon soy sauce

In a skillet or wok, fry bacon until crisp, and remove. To the bacon drippings, add onion, cabbage, cayenne, ginger, and soy. Cook over medium heat until the cabbage and onions are very soft and wilted. Add the crumbled bacon, and stir. Serves 4.

Domino Carrot Casserole

2½ cups sliced carrots
Boiling water
3   teaspoons chicken bouillon
1   large onion, chopped
¼   cup margarine
2   cups soft bread crumbs

½   teaspoon salt
½   cup sharp Cheddar cheese,
    grated
2   tablespoons water
Extra margarine

Cook carrots in boiling water with the chicken bouillon until just tender; drain. In a skillet, sauté onion in the ¼ cup of margarine. Add bread crumbs, salt, cheese, and water; mix well. In a greased 1-quart casserole, place 1 cup of the cooked carrots; cover with the bread crumb mixture. Place the remaining carrots in fallen domino fashion, beginning at the edge of the casserole. Use the extra margarine to dot the top. Bake at 350° for 20 to 25 minutes. Serves 6.

Leonard's Spicy Carrot Casserole

8-9 medium carrots
2 tablespoons grated onion
2 tablespoons bottled
  horseradish
½ cup mayonnaise

1 teaspoon salt
½ teaspoon pepper
⅓ cup buttered bread crumbs
Paprika

Scrape carrots, and cut into sticks; cook in salted water until tender. Combine onion, horseradish, mayonnaise, salt, and pepper. Spread the cooked carrots in the bottom of a greased baking dish; cover carrots with the sauce. Sprinkle bread crumbs on sauce, and top with paprika for color. Bake at 375° for 15-20 minutes. Serves 6.

Eggplant Sticks Parmesan

1 medium eggplant
Salt
Self-rising corn meal

Vegetable oil
Parmesan cheese, grated

Peel eggplant, and cut into sticks like carrot sticks. Place the sticks into a bowl, and salt. Allow the salted sticks to stand for 20 minutes. Pat the sticks dry. Place corn meal and the dried sticks into a plastic bag; shake to coat the sticks with the meal. Place the coated sticks on a cookie sheet and freeze for about 15-20 minutes. In a large skillet, heat oil to high; drop coated sticks into the oil. Reduce heat to medium, and fry until eggplant is cooked and browned. Drain very carefully on paper towel; also gently pat tops to absorb excess oil. Add a light sprinkling of salt and a heavy sprinkling of Parmesan. Allow to cool and crisp before serving. Do not cover or stack.

It's incredible—kids like this vegetable. Take care not to mention that it's a vegetable, though!

Corn, Okra, and Tomatoes

2 tablespoons margarine
1 medium onion, chopped
2 tablespoons green pepper, chopped
1 pound okra, sliced
1½ cups water

¾ cup canned tomatoes, chopped
2 or 3 ears of corn, slice kernels off cob
1 drop Tabasco sauce
Salt and pepper to taste

In a large skillet, melt margarine, and sauté onion and green pepper until tender. Add okra, water, and tomatoes; cook on medium heat, covered for 15 minutes. Add more water as needed as cooking progresses. Stir in corn and Tabasco; continue to cook on simmer for 10 minutes. Salt and pepper to taste; then cook, uncovered, for another 15 minutes. Serves 6.

Corn Pudding

2 eggs, well beaten
1 teaspoon sugar
1½ tablespoons plain flour
2 tablespoons margarine, melted

½ cup milk
1 (16-ounce) can white cream style corn
Pepper to taste
½ teaspoon salt

Combine all ingredients, and mix well. Pour into a well-greased 1½-quart casserole. Bake at 300° for 1 hour and 15 minutes. Stir the ingredients once when mixture begins to thicken to prevent the corn from sticking on bottom of casserole. Serves 6.

Scotty's Eggplant Casserole

2 medium eggplants
Salt
1 green pepper, minced
1 medium onion, minced
1 tablespoon bacon drippings
1 egg, beaten

1 cup Ritz cracker crumbs
2 to 4 drops Tabasco sauce
¼ teaspoon pepper
1 cup sharp Cheddar cheese, grated
½ cup Parmesan cheese, grated

Peel eggplant, cut into pieces, and salt. Allow to stand for 20 minutes. Cook in boiling salted water until very tender; drain and mash. Sauté green pepper and onion in the bacon drippings until tender. Remove from heat. Stir in the eggplant, egg, cracker crumbs, Tabasco sauce, and pepper. Salt to taste. In a greased 1½-quart casserole, spoon ½ eggplant mixture; cover with the Cheddar cheese. Spoon remaining eggplant mixture over Cheddar cheese, and top with the Parmesan cheese. Bake at 350° for 30 minutes. Serves 6.

Italian Towers

1 medium eggplant, with no green on skin
Salt
1 large fresh tomato, sliced
1 large mild onion, sliced thin
½ cup margarine

½ teaspoon basil
4 slices Mozzarella cheese, 2½ inches square
½ cup Italian bread crumbs
2 tablespoons Parmesan cheese, grated

Preheat oven to 450°. Peel eggplant and slice ½- to ¾-inches thick. Soak in cold, salted water for 15 minutes. Drain on paper towel, and pat dry. In a flat, greased 2-quart baking dish, place four slices of eggplant, lightly salted on both sides. Cover each slice with a salted slice of both tomato and onion. Melt ¼ cup margarine, and pour evenly over the four towers. Sprinkle with basil, and bake, covered, in a preheated oven at 450° for 20 minutes. Place a slice of Mozzarella cheese over each tower. Combine bread crumbs and remaining ¼ cup margarine and sprinkle on top of Mozzarella. Finally, top with the Parmesan cheese. Bake, uncovered, for about 8 minutes or until cheese is bubbly. Serves 4.

Creole Eggplant

1 large eggplant, with no green on skin	1 cup canned tomatoes
¼ cup celery, minced	½ cup sharp Cheddar cheese, grated
1 small onion, minced	1 tablespoon parsley flakes
1 small green pepper, minced	1 teaspoon baking powder
2 tablespoons margarine	1 cup cracker crumbs, divided
1 egg, beaten	Salt to taste

Peel eggplant, and slice into a bowl of salted water; let soak for 15-20 minutes. Pour off water, and boil eggplant in fresh, salted water until very tender; drain and mash. Sauté celery, onion and green pepper in margarine; then stir in eggplant, egg, tomatoes, cheese, parsley flakes, baking powder, and ½ the cracker crumbs. Mix well, salt to taste, and pour into a greased 1½-quart casserole; top with remaining cracker crumbs. Bake at 350° for 40 minutes.

Fried Plantains

Plantains are a type of large banana used for frying. Buy them ripe with black spots on them, and **do not** refrigerate. Peel plantains, and slice on a slight diagonal; cook in medium-hot vegetable oil until golden brown. Drain well and serve. They will be naturally sweet.

Scalloped Pineapple

Prepare 1 day before serving.

½ cup margarine	2 (16-ounce) cans pineapple chunks, drained
1 cup sugar	2 cups milk
2 eggs	4 cups cubed bread (5 slices)

In an electric mixer, cream margarine and sugar. Add eggs; beat well. Add pineapple, milk, and bread cubes; mix well. Pour into a greased casserole. Cover and refrigerate overnight. Bake uncovered at 350° for 1½-2 hours or until well set.

Terry's Gnocchi

3 cups water	½ teaspoon pepper
1 cup raw, quick grits	1 cup Swiss cheese, grated
1½ cups milk	⅓ cup melted butter
4 tablespoons butter	½ cup Parmesan cheese
Salt to taste	

In a large saucepan, boil water; slowly add grits, then stir vigorously. Cover and cook on medium high heat until grits begin to thicken. Stir in milk, and re-cover. Continue to cook slowly for about 5 minutes more. Add the 4 tablespoons butter, salt, and pepper. Pour hot grits into an electric mixer bowl, and beat on high speed for 5 minutes. Add Swiss cheese, and mix to blend. Pour grits into a greased, flat casserole, and refrigerate to allow grits to chill and become firm. When grits are very firm, cut into 2-inch squares, and place in fallen domino fashion in a greased, flat casserole. Pour the melted ⅓ cup butter over the squares, and sprinkle with Parmesan cheese. Bake at 400° for 25 to 30 minutes or until bubbling. Serves 6-8.

If you are wondering about the pronunciation of the recipe, try "no-she." This recipe will make a grits lover of anyone. Don't be surprised if your dominos fall down. The heating process causes that to happen, so the Parmesan cheese can be blended during the cooking.

Ann's Dressing

3 cups self-rising corn meal
2 medium onions, chopped
½ cup bacon drippings or
   vegetable oil
6 eggs, divided

¾ cup milk
8 slices toasted white bread
Water
About 3¾ cups chicken or
   turkey stock
1½ teaspoons black pepper

Preheat oven to 350°. Combine corn meal and onions. Heat drippings until hot, but not smoking. Pour hot drippings into corn meal mixture, and beat vigorously. Add 3 well-beaten eggs, and the milk to the mixture; mix well. Pour into a greased baking pan, and bake in a preheated oven at 350° until browned. While corn bread is baking, place the toast in a large bowl, and add just enough water to cover the toast. Soak toast for a few minutes; then drain off water, and squeeze water out of bread. When corn bread is cooked, crumble it into the bowl with the wet toast; mix well. Add chicken stock, and black pepper. Beat in the remaining 3 eggs, and mix thoroughly. Pour into a greased baking pan. Bake at 350° until browned and set, about 35 minutes.

Dressing can be made a day ahead of serving, and refrigerated until baking time. Uncooked dressing can be frozen. Thaw before baking.

Madie's Vegetable Casserole

2 (10-ounce) boxes frozen
   mixed vegetables
1 cup celery, chopped
1 cup onion, chopped
1 cup mayonnaise
1 cup grated sharp Cheddar
   cheese, divided

Salt to taste
Pepper to taste
½ teaspoon celery seed
2 cups bite-size Nabisco
   Cheese Crackers (Nips),
   crushed
¼ cup melted margarine

Cook vegetables as directed on package; drain. Combine celery, onions, mayonnaise, ½ cup of the cheese, salt, pepper, and celery seed; then mix into the cooked vegetables. Spoon into a well-greased baking dish. Mix together Nips, melted margarine, and remaining ½ cup cheese. Sprinkle over top of casserole. Bake at 350° for 30-40 minutes. Serves 8.

Baked Onions

1 medium onion per person	¼ teaspoon Worcestershire
Heavy aluminium foil	sauce per onion
	Salt and pepper

Cut a thin slice off the **top** (not stem) of the onion; then carefully peel off all outside skin. Quarter onion, stopping ¼-inch short of the stem. Spread the onion slightly, taking care not to split apart. Cut a piece of foil larger than the onion. Place onion, stem side down, in center of foil, and form foil into a "cup" around the onion. Sprinkle the Worcestershire sauce into the cut onion; then salt and lightly pepper. Close top of foil and give a tight twist. Take care not to puncture foil package. Place foil packages in a shallow pan, and bake at 350° for 45 minutes or until packages are soft when squeezed. These packages can also be cooked on the grill or in the coals of a fire.

Genia's Baked Vermicelli and Cheese

1½ cups vermicelli (break vermicelli in half and stand on end in measuring cup to measure)	2 eggs, well beaten
	½ cup milk
	2 cups sharp Cheddar cheese, grated
¼ cup margarine	Extra cheese for top
Salt and pepper to taste	

Cook vermicelli according to package directions; do not overcook. Drain; then add margarine, salt, and pepper. In a small bowl, combine beaten eggs, milk, and cheese; mix well. Pour egg mixture over hot vermicelli, and toss to mix. Pour vermicelli mixture into a greased casserole. Top with extra cheese. Bake at 350° for about 35 minutes or until liquid is set. Serves 4-6.

Hong Kong Peas

½ pound bacon slices
1 medium onion, minced
1 (4-ounce) can sliced
mushrooms, drained
1 (17-ounce) can English peas,
undrained

1 teaspoon garlic salt
1 drop Tabasco sauce
2 tablespoons Worcestershire
sauce
1 teaspoon MSG

Fry bacon until crisp, and remove from skillet to drain. Sauté onions and mushrooms in a small amount of the bacon drippings. Pour peas and their liquid into a saucepan; add the sautéed mixture with a little of the drippings. Crumble crisp bacon into the peas; add garlic salt, Tabasco sauce, Worcestershire sauce, and MSG. Bring peas to a boil; stir and reduce heat to simmer. Cook, uncovered, for 45 minutes. The liquid will thicken, and the peas will get wrinkled. Great! That's what makes them taste good. Serves 4.

A very different English pea recipe. Perhaps you'll like this Far East flavor.

Blackeyed Peas Deluxe

2 (16-ounce) cans blackeyed
peas
1½ ounces pepperoni, diced

1 medium green pepper,
minced
1 medium onion, minced
1 teaspoon hot taco sauce

Combine all ingredients in a saucepan; stir. Simmer for 1 hour. Serves 6.

The different ethnic flavors of Italy and Mexico blend, and add a very special flavor to this already ethnic food. Simple and delicious.

Macaroni and Cheese Casserole

1 (8-ounce) package elbow macaroni
1 (10¾-ounce) can mushroom soup
1 small onion, minced
1 (2-ounce) jar pimento, minced

¼ teaspoon salt
1 cup mayonnaise
1 cup sharp Cheddar cheese, grated
½ cup crushed cracker crumbs

Cook macaroni as directed on the package; drain. Place macaroni in a large mixing bowl. Stir in all other ingredients except the cracker crumbs; mix well. Place mixture into a greased 2-quart casserole. Top with the cracker crumbs. Bake at 400° for about 30 minutes.

Vermicelli Toss

8 ounces vermicelli, broken in half
1 tablespoon margarine
6 ounces sour cream
1 cup sharp Cheddar cheese, grated

1 clove garlic, crushed
1 teaspoon coarse ground black pepper
Salt to taste

Add vermicelli to 2-quarts of salted, boiling water, and stir. Bring back to a boil; cover with a lid, and turn heat off. Leave pot on burner, and let it steep for exactly 9 minutes; drain. In a saucepan, melt margarine; then add the hot, drained vermicelli, sour cream, cheese, garlic, and pepper. Toss gently until all ingredients are mixed and melted. Return to low heat, stirring constantly until heated completely. Add salt if needed. Serves 4.

This is a favorite with adults and children. Quick and delicious. Reheats easily in microwave.

Beverly's Melt-In-Your-Mouth Potato Casserole

4 or 5 medium Irish potatoes
1   medium onion, chopped
Salt and pepper

1   cup sharp Cheddar cheese, grated
½   pint whipping cream

Boil unpeeled potatoes in unsalted water until tender. Allow potatoes to cool; then peel, and grate on the coarse side of a box-type grater (do not slice.) In a greased 2-quart baking dish, make a layer of ½ the potatoes and ½ the onions; then salt and pepper. Repeat with remaining potatoes and onions. Salt and pepper again, fairly heavily. Sprinkle cheese evenly over the top, and pour cream over all as evenly as possible. Cover with aluminium foil, and bake at 350° for 45 minutes. Serves 4.

So simple, yet outstanding. The whipping cream and cheese do wonderful things for the potatoes. Not so wonderful for the waistline, but . . .

Potatoes Cecelia

1   (2-pound) package frozen
     hash brown potatoes
½   cup onion, minced
2   tablespoons margarine
1   (10¾-ounce) can cream of
     chicken soup

16 ounces sour cream
12 ounces sharp Cheddar
     cheese, grated
Salt and pepper to taste
½   cup margarine

Allow the hash brown potatoes to completely thaw; drain thoroughly. Sauté the onion in the 2 tablespoons of margarine until tender. Combine the thawed, drained potatoes with the soup, sour cream, cheese, salt, and pepper; mix well. Melt the ½ cup of margarine in a 3-quart baking dish; then pour the potato mixture into the baking dish over the melted margarine. Bake at 350° for 35-45 minutes or until bubbling. Serves 10-12.

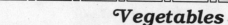

Potatoes Baronne

½ cup margarine, softened	4 large baking potatoes,
1 envelope Lipton's Onion	unpeeled
Soup Mix	

Mix margarine with soup mix until creamy. Scrub unpeeled potatoes, and make four cuts across the potato (do not cut completely through). Generously fill each cut with margarine mixture. Force the mixture deeply into the cuts with a flat blade knife. Wrap each potato in heavy aluminum foil, and bake in oven at 350° or on the grill until potatoes are soft and done, about an hour. Serves 4.

Mildred's German Potato Salad, Bavarian Style

3 pounds small red potatoes	Salt and pepper to taste
5 slices bacon	3 tablespoons sour cream
1 large white onion, chopped	3 tablespoons mayonnaise
2 tablespoons white vinegar	

Boil unpeeled potatoes in salted water until tender; drain, and keep hot. Chop bacon; fry slowly until crisp. Add onions and vinegar to bacon and the drippings. Keep bacon mixture warm. Peel potatoes, and toss gently with bacon mixture. Add salt and pepper to taste. Combine sour cream and mayonnaise; mix gently into the potato salad. Add more sour cream and mayonnaise mixture, if desired. Serve hot. Serves 6.

Hash Brown Wedges

3 medium potatoes, unpeeled
2 tablespoons onion, grated
1 teaspoon salt

Dash pepper
¼ cup margarine or bacon
  drippings, divided

Boil or microwave unpeeled potatoes until soft; then chill. When chilled, peel potatoes, and grate. Add onion, salt, and pepper; mix well. Melt 2 tablespoons of the margarine or drippings in a 10-inch non-stick skillet. Pat potato mixture into skillet, leaving a ½-inch space around the edge. Brown on medium heat for about 9 minutes; heat may need to be reduced. Cut into 4 wedges; remove from skillet. Melt remaining 2 tablespoons margarine; then return wedges to skillet, uncooked side down. Brown for about 7 minutes more. Serves 4.

Rice Consommé

3 tablespoons margarine
1 cup raw regular rice

2 (10-ounce) cans consommé
4 ounces mushrooms, drained

In a large skillet, melt margarine; add rice and cook, stirring, until rice is a very light brown or translucent color. Slowly add both cans of consommé to the hot rice; then add mushrooms. Bring to a boil; then cover, and reduce heat. Simmer for 12 minutes exactly; then uncover and remove from heat. Rice will still appear very juicy. Set aside for 10 minutes to finish cooking. Serves 6.

This is the quickest, easiest dish around the house, and one of the tastiest. Keep all ingredients on hand, and you can have it ready in a hurry for unexpected guests or for the family. If there are "mushroom objectors" around, just leave out the mushrooms. It tastes just as good.

Spanish Rice

1½ cups raw regular rice
¼ cup oil
1 large onion, minced
1 green pepper, minced
2 large tomatoes, finely chopped
2 drops Tabasco sauce
2 tablespoons parsley, minced

1 teaspoon ground cumin
2 small cloves garlic, minced
3 cups water
2 teaspoons salt
½ teaspoon pepper
1 cup sharp Cheddar cheese, grated

In a skillet, sauté rice in the oil until light brown. Add onion, and continue to cook until onion is limp. Add remaining ingredients except cheese. Transfer rice mixture to a greased casserole, and bake, covered, at 350° for 1 hour. Just before serving, stir the cheese into the hot rice and mix until melted; serve hot. Serves 8-10.

Spinach Madeline

2 (10-ounce) packages frozen chopped spinach
4 tablespoons margarine
2 tablespoons plain flour
2 tablespoons onion, chopped
½ cup evaporated milk
¾ teaspoon celery salt

1 teaspoon Worcestershire sauce
¾ teaspoon garlic powder
1 (6-ounce) roll jalapeño pepper cheese, cubed
Buttered bread crumbs

Cook spinach according to directions on the package, omitting the salt. Drain in a bowl to reserve ½ cup spinach liquid. In a skillet, melt margarine, and add flour and onion. Stir until smooth; then gradually add the ½ cup reserved spinach liquid and the milk. Cook, while stirring constantly, until thickened. Stir in celery salt, Worcestershire sauce, garlic powder, and cubed cheese until melted and blended. Add spinach and mix well. Pour into a greased 2-quart baking dish, and cover with bread crumbs. Bake at 350° for 30 minutes.

No bland spinach here! This is hot, spicy, and very good.

Cheesy Squash Casserole

2 pounds yellow summer squash	2 eggs, well beaten
1 medium onion, minced	2 cups sharp Cheddar cheese, grated
1 teaspoon garlic salt	Buttered cracker crumbs
¼ teaspoon pepper	Paprika
2 slices bread	

Cook squash in salted water until very tender; draining as much water out as possible. Mash squash thoroughly; then add onion, garlic salt, pepper, and bread slices. Let bread slices absorb any extra liquid from the squash (add another slice of bread, if needed). Stir in beaten eggs, and mix well; then stir in the cheese. Blend cheese throughout the mixture. Pour into a greased 2-quart baking dish. Top with cracker crumbs, and sprinkle with paprika. Bake at 350° for 30 minutes.

If serving this dish for a special occasion, omit the cracker crumbs, and be creative with cheese slices and spices. The color of the squash lends itself to a large single daisy of cheese with green parsley flakes as leaves and grass, then a touch of paprika in the center of the daisy for color.

Squash Maximilian

2 pounds yellow summer squash	1 large onion, sliced in rings
8 slices bacon	1 roll jalapeño cheese, cubed
	Cracker crumbs

Cut squash into pieces, and boil in unsalted water; drain completely. Fry bacon until crisp, and remove from skillet. Brown onion rings in some of the bacon drippings. In a greased casserole, make layers beginning with drained squash, crumbled bacon, onion rings, and cheese cubes. Repeat layers; then top with cracker crumbs. Bake at 325° for 40 minutes. Serves 10.

Squash Marjo

5 medium yellow summer squash, sliced	½ teaspoon black pepper
¼ cup margarine, melted	4 teaspoons sugar
½ cup mayonnaise	¼ cup green pepper, minced
1 egg, slightly beaten	½ cup grated sharp Cheddar cheese, divided
1 teaspoon salt	½ cup bread crumbs, divided

Cook squash in salted boiling water until tender; drain very well, and mash. Mix together melted margarine, mayonnaise, egg, salt, black pepper, sugar, green pepper, ¼ cup of the cheese, and ¼ cup of the bread crumbs. Pour into greased 1½-quart casserole; top with remaining cheese and bread crumbs. Bake at 350° for 45 minutes or until light brown and bubbly. Serves 4-6.

This is a great recipe for using a food processor. In order to save washing and drying the bowl, make bread crumbs with steel blade; remove to a side bowl. Then change blades to the cheese grater, and grate cheese; remove to a side bowl. Change blade back to the steel one, and chop the green pepper; then add the cooked squash to be mashed. Continue with recipe as stated above.

Squash Puppies

5	medium yellow summer squash	½	cup self-rising corn meal
1	small onion, minced	2	tablespoons plain flour
¾	cup sharp Cheddar cheese, grated	1	egg, well beaten

Cook squash in salted, boiling water until very tender; drain well. Completely mash squash, and add onion, cheese, corn meal, flour, and egg. Mix until blended and the consistency of hush puppies or croquettes. More corn meal may be needed, but do not get mixture stiff. Fry in medium-hot vegetable oil until cooked through and browned. Drain well on paper towel. This mixture can be made and refrigerated, then cooked anytime within 3 days.

A fantastic way to hide squash from the children. They'll go for hush puppies, but not **squash!** *To salve your conscience, casually mention, when the kids are about 25, that the recipe has* **squash** *in it. That ought to make you feel better.*

Tasty Quick Spinach

| 1 | can (15-ounce) spinach, drained | 2 | teaspoons soy sauce |
| ¼ | teaspoon garlic salt | 1 | tablespoon margarine |

Place drained spinach in a small saucepan, and add all other ingredients. Stir to mix. Heat spinach until boiling; reduce heat to simmer. Cook for 5 minutes. Serves 3-4.

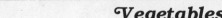
Baked Squash Boats

8 medium summer yellow squash	1 cup croutons, crushed
Salt and pepper to taste	½ teaspoon garlic salt
¼ cup green pepper, minced	1 egg, beaten
½ cup onion, minced	1 cup sharp Cheddar cheese,
1 tablespoon vegetable oil	grated
	Paprika

Boil whole squash in salted water for about 20 minutes or until tender. Drain squash, and allow to cool for 15 minutes. Split the whole squash in half lengthwise. Scoop out the center to make a cavity, leaving enough pulp to allow squash to retain its shape. Place the squash "boats" on a greased cookie sheet, and salt very lightly. Sauté green pepper and onion in the oil until limp. Stir in the squash pulp, and mash thoroughly while mixing with green pepper and onion. Add crushed croutons and garlic salt. Salt and pepper to taste. Mix in the beaten egg and cheese until well blended. Spoon squash filling into the "boats," and sprinkle with paprika. Bake at 350° for about 20-25 minutes. Serves 8-10.

Lucy's Turnip Greens Southern Style

3 pounds tender turnip greens	3 cups water
2 ounces salt pork or fat back	Salt to taste
3 or 4 tablespoons bacon drippings	Pinch of sugar

Shake turnip greens outside vigorously. Remove any large stems from the greens; then wash in **many** changes of cold water until all the leaves are thoroughly clean. In a Dutch oven, place the salt pork, bacon drippings, and water and boil for about 10 minutes. Add turnip greens; bring back to a boil, cover, and simmer for about 1½ hours. Check during the cooking time for salt. After 1½ hours of cooking add the pinch of sugar and stir. Serve hot with cornbread.

Turnip greens, corn bread, and "pot licker"—kinda like dying and going to heaven for this "soul food."

Broiled Tomatoes with Oil and Mustard

6 firm, ripe, medium tomatoes	4 tablespoons brown sugar
6 tablespoons vegetable oil	2 tablespoons onion, minced
1½ teaspoons salt	2 teaspoons vinegar
2 teaspoons prepared mustard	Cracker crumbs

Cut a thin slice from the top (not stem) side of the tomatoes, and slightly hollow the centers of the tomatoes. Mix all ingredients together except the tomatoes and crumbs. Place 2 teaspoons of this dressing mixture in each hollow. Sprinkle the tops with cracker crumbs. Drizzle a little of the dressing over the crumbs. Place the tomatoes in a greased shallow baking dish; broil under moderate heat for about 10 minutes or until tomatoes are tender. Baste 3 times during broiling with the dressing. Serves 6.

For a variation of this recipe, follow directions but omit the crumbs. Cook for 8 minutes; then remove tomatoes from oven, and stir center of tomatoes while adding cooked rice. Cover with the crumbs and bake again for about 5 minutes or until rice is hot and crumbs browned.

Baked Cheese-Stuffed Tomatoes

1 tablespoon margarine	1 tablespoon grated onion
¼ cup soft bread crumbs	4 large ripe unpeeled
⅓ cup sharp Cheddar cheese, grated	tomatoes, washed

Melt margarine; add bread crumbs, cheese, and onion. Quarter tomatoes, cutting ⅔ of the way down. Stuff center of tomatoes with bread crumb mixture. Wrap each tomato in aluminum foil, seal, and place in a baking pan. Bake at 350° for 20 to 30 minutes. Serves 4.

Dawn's Zucchini and Onion Crêpe Tower

Crêpes: 10 to 12 crêpes will be needed. Make 8-inch crêpes (see Breads) and set aside.

Filling:

3 tablespoons margarine, divided	2 pounds unpeeled zucchini, shredded
3 tablespoons vegetable oil, divided	2 tablespoons parsley, chopped
4 large onions, sliced in thin rings	1½ teaspoons oregano
	1½ teaspoons salt
	¼ teaspoon pepper

Sauce:

2 tablespoons margarine	2 eggs, well beaten
3 tablespoons plain flour	¼ cup Parmesan cheese and an extra amount for garnish
½ teaspoon salt	Paprika
1½ cups milk	

To make filling, heat in a skillet 2 tablespoons of the margarine and 2 tablespoons of the oil; add onions. Sauté until tender, stirring often, for about 10 minutes. Remove onions with a slotted spoon into a bowl. Add remaining margarine and oil to the skillet; heat and add zucchini. Cook on high, stirring often, until zucchini is tender and juices have evaporated. This should take 5-10 minutes; do not brown. Add onions to the skillet along with parsley, oregano, salt, and pepper. Set aside.

To make sauce, melt margarine in a skillet; stir in flour and salt. Gradually stir in the milk, and continue stirring over medium heat until sauce is thickened. Very slowly, while beating vigorously, add ½ the sauce to the beaten eggs. Return sauce with egg in it to the skillet, and add the cheese; stir until well blended. Measure and reserve 1 cup of sauce.

To assemble, use an oversize pie dish, and grease well. Crêpes will be stacked flat. Place one crêpe on the bottom of dish; then add ⅓ cup filling, and spread over the crêpe evenly. Top with 2 tablespoons sauce; spread evenly. Repeat layers of crêpe, filling, and sauce. Top tower with a plain crêpe; then pour the reserved 1 cup of sauce over it. Sprinkle with Parmesan cheese and paprika. Bake at 350° for 30 minutes. Let tower cool for a few minutes; then cut like a pie. Serves 8-10.

Breads and Sweet Breads

Frances's Old Fashioned Homemade Rolls

1 (¼-ounce) package active dry yeast	½ cup sugar
¼ cup lukewarm water	1 cup boiling water
¼ cup solid shortening	1 egg, beaten
1¼ teaspoons salt	3½ cups plain flour, sifted

Preheat oven to 375° about 15 minutes before cooking time. Dissolve yeast in lukewarm water, and set aside. In a large mixing bowl, place shortening, salt, and sugar; then add the boiling water. Stir until sugar and shortening are **completely** dissolved; let cool. When mixture is just warm, add yeast and egg; mix well. Gradually stir in the flour, and beat until smooth. Cover bowl with a plate, and refrigerate for 2 to 24 hours. The dough will be a little sticky to use, so place ⅓ dough on a floured surface, and sift a small amount of flour on top of dough. Pat with hands to ½-inch thickness, and cut with a 3-inch cutter. Place rolls in greased pie pans with the sides touching. Repeat with remaining dough until all rolls are made. Let rolls rise in a warm place for 1 hour. Bake rolls in a preheated oven at 375° on the second rack from the top of the oven for about 10 minutes. Carefully watch rolls on the bottom as well as the top. After cooling, the rolls freeze well. Wrap in foil packages of 8 to 10 rolls and seal carefully; then place in Ziploc bags to freeze. Yield: about 21 rolls.

Somehow when I make rolls, my kitchen always looks like the first light snowfall of winter. Perhaps I should consider turning off the ceiling fan? Then it would only be me looking like a snowman. Kitchen destruction aside, these are wonderful rolls to make for that special occasion or person.

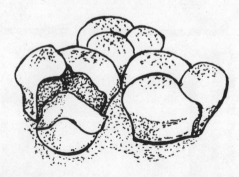

Angel Biscuits

2 (¼-ounce) packages dry yeast
5 tablespoons lukewarm water
5½ to 6 cups plain flour
1 teaspoon soda
3 teaspoons baking powder
1 teaspoon salt
4 tablespoons sugar
1 cup vegetable shortening
2 cups buttermilk

Preheat oven to 400°. Dissolve yeast in the lukewarm water; set aside. Measure flour and sift; then re-measure flour, and sift with soda, baking powder, salt, and sugar. Cut the shortening into the flour mixture until evenly distributed; add yeast and buttermilk. Blend very well. Let dough rest for 30 minutes; then roll on a floured surface, and cut out with a 3-3½-inch cutter. Bake at 400° in a preheated oven for 10-12 minutes. Yield: 32.

To make a smaller number of biscuits, use 3 cups flour, and cut all other ingredients in half. The biscuits are truly well-named since they taste heavenly!

Biscuits

2 cups plain flour
1 teaspoon baking powder
½ teaspoon salt
3 tablespoons vegetable shortening
½ cup sweet milk or buttermilk

Preheat oven to 400°. Sift together the flour, baking powder, and salt into a bowl. Cut the shortening into the flour mixture with a fork. Stir in the milk, and mix well. Knead the dough for a few minutes. Roll out on a floured surface to ½ to ¾ inch thickness. Cut biscuits out with a cutter, and place on a greased pan. Bake in a preheated oven at 400° until biscuits are lightly browned on top. Yield: 10-12 biscuits.

Petite Sour Cream Rolls

1 cup sour cream	2 cups self-rising flour
1 cup margarine, melted	

Preheat oven to 350° about 15 minutes before baking time. Mix all ingredients, and spoon into petite muffin pans that have been greased. The dough can be made and refrigerated two days before using. Bake at 350° for about 15 minutes.

Swiss French Bread

¾ cup margarine, melted	2 teaspoons seasoned salt
8 green onions, chopped	1 loaf fresh French bread,
2 teaspoons lemon juice	sliced **lengthwise**
2 teaspoons poppy seeds	1 pound Swiss cheese, grated
2 teaspoons Dijon mustard	

Melt margarine; add green onions, lemon juice, poppy seeds, mustard, and seasoned salt. Mix until well-blended. Spread on both halves of the French bread. Top the margarine mixture with ½ pound grated cheese on each loaf half. Place both halves side by side on aluminum foil; do **not** cover. Bake at 350° for 20 minutes.

Can be served as bread at a meal or cut into smaller pieces and served as appetizers.

Bubba's Hush Puppies

¼ cup self-rising flour	⅔ tablespoon vegetable oil
1 egg, beaten	1 cup self-rising corn meal
½ cup buttermilk	½ cup onion, minced

Mix all ingredients until well blended. Form into hush puppies, and fry in vegetable oil until brown and cooked through. Drain well on paper towel. Do not stack or cover.

Corn Bread

2 tablespoons bacon drippings, divided	1 cup buttermilk
1 cup self-rising corn meal	2 eggs, well-beaten

Preheat oven to 450°. Place the bacon drippings in a 6-inch iron skillet, and heat until very hot, but not smoking. Combine corn meal, buttermilk, and beaten eggs; mix well. Pour 1 tablespoon of the hot bacon drippings into the batter, and beat until well-mixed. Tilt the skillet with remaining bacon drippings to coat the skillet. Immediately pour batter into skillet. Bake in a preheated oven at 450° for 30 to 35 minutes.

Do not make batter and let it stand. Batter should be baked as soon as it is made. If your corn meal is plain rather than self-rising, add 1 teaspoon baking powder and ¼ teaspoon salt to the batter.

Basic Crêpes

2 cups plain flour	1 cup cold water
½ teaspoon salt	4 tablespoons margarine, melted
4 large eggs	
1 cup milk	Vegetable oil

In a food processor or a blender, combine flour, salt, eggs, milk, water, and melted margarine. Blend until completely mixed. Pour batter into a glass bowl, and refrigerate for at least 2 hours. Pour a few drops of oil into the bottom of 2 8-inch skillets, and coat bottom. Heat skillets over medium heat; then pour a scant ¼ cup batter into 1 skillet. Quickly tilt the skillet in all directions, causing the batter to coat the bottom. Pour off excess batter to reuse. Cook for about 1 minute. Shake to loosen crêpe; then flip the crêpe, uncooked side down, into the other skillet. Cook for about ½ minute. Discard the first crêpe made, and continue making crêpes with as little oil as possible. The second side cooked is the side to place filling on, if rolling the crêpe, since the first side cooked looks best. Yield: about 20-28 crêpes.

Make crêpes in advance, and stack, after cooling, between sheets of waxed paper. Refrigerate or freeze until ready to use. Very handy to have a stack frozen to use for a quick main dish, or a light dessert.

Baby Buffins

1 cup self-rising flour
3 level tablespoons
   commercial mayonnaise

½ cup milk

Preheat oven to 400°. Combine self-rising flour and mayonnaise. Gradually stir in the milk until just blended. Place the batter into greased mini muffin pans. Bake in a preheated 400° oven for 12 to 15 minutes or until very light brown.

Mexican Corn Bread

1½ cups plain corn meal
1 teaspoon salt
3 teaspoons baking powder
2 eggs, beaten
⅔ cup vegetable oil

1 cup sour cream
2 tablespoons jalapeño relish
1 (16-ounce) can cream-style
   corn
1 cup sharp Cheddar cheese,
   grated

Preheat oven to 350°. Combine corn meal, salt, and baking powder; mix well. Add eggs, oil, and sour cream; stir until mixture is just blended. Stir in jalapeño relish and corn. Pour ½ batter into a greased 8-inch square baking dish. Cover with ½ of the cheese; repeat layers of batter and cheese. Bake in a preheated oven at 350° for 35 to 40 minutes. Cut into squares.

Buttermilk Waffles

1½ cups plain flour
1   tablespoon corn meal
½   teaspoon salt
2   teaspoons baking powder

½   teaspoon soda
1   cup buttermilk
1   egg, beaten
½   cup vegetable oil

Sift flour, corn meal, salt, and baking powder together. Mix soda into buttermilk; then add to dry mixture. Stir in the beaten egg and the oil; mix very well. Refrigerate batter until ready to use.

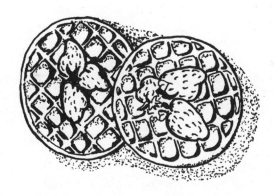

Sweet Breads

Danish Pinwheel Rolls

1 package dry yeast	¼ cup solid shortening
¼ cup warm water	1 teaspoon salt
¼ cup sugar	3½ cups plain flour
1 cup milk	1 large egg, beaten

Filling:

6 tablespoons margarine, very soft	⅔ cup sugar
	2 teaspoons cinnamon

Preheat oven to 375° about 15 minutes before baking rolls. Sprinkle the yeast on the warm water, and set aside. In a small saucepan, heat sugar, milk, shortening, and salt until sugar is dissolved and shortening is barely melted. Add ½ of the flour, and blend well; then add the yeast mixture and egg. Stir until blended; add remaining flour, and mix well. Place dough on a floured surface, and knead until smooth and elastic, about 10 minutes. Place in a greased bowl, cover, and allow to rise in a warm place until double in size, about 2 hours. Punch the dough down, and shape into a ball; then cover and allow dough to rest 10 minutes. On a floured surface, roll dough into a 10×18 inch rectangle, about ½-inch thick. Mix the filling ingredients, and spread over the rectangle evenly. Beginning at the wide side, roll jellyroll style, and seal seam and ends; then cut in 1 inch slices. Grease round baking pans, and place the rolls cut side down.

Allow rolls to touch, but do not crowd since they will rise. Cover and allow to rise in a warm place for about 45 minutes. They should be about double in size. Bake in a preheated oven at 375° for 15 to 20 minutes or until done. Yield: 18.

The consumption rate on these rolls boggles the mind. You might as well take the extra time, and make 2 or 3 batches while you're at it. Make batches separately; do not double the recipe. Freeze some, and give some as gifts.

Stay Up All Night Coffee Cake

¾ cup nuts, chopped
1 package frozen Parker House rolls
1 (3¾-ounce) package instant or regular butterscotch pudding mix

½ cup brown sugar
½ cup margarine, melted
Cinnamon to taste

Grease a Bundt pan; then sprinkle with the chopped nuts on bottom of the pan. Arrange rolls evenly over the nuts. Sprinkle dry pudding over the rolls. In a small bowl, combine sugar, melted margarine, and cinnamon. Cover rolls with the sugar mixture. Place in a **cold oven** to remain overnight. In the morning, remove rolls from the oven; then preheat oven to 350°. Return rolls to oven, and bake for 25 minutes. Serves 10 to 12.

Can't wait until I have a "Kitchybot" (kitchen robot); then it can take the rolls out of the oven, make the juice and coffee, and bake the rolls when the oven is ready. Let's not stop there. Kitchybot, do you serve breakfast in bed? Dream on . . .

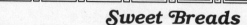

Sweet Breads

Williamsburg Cranberry Pecan Muffins

Cranberries require overnight preparation.

1 cup cranberries	1 egg, well beaten
¾ cup sugar, divided	¾ cup buttermilk
2 cups plain flour	¼ cup solid shortening, melted
¼ teaspoon salt	½ cup pecans, chopped
¾ teaspoon soda	

Preheat oven to 400° about 15 minutes before baking time. Chop cranberries in a food processor with the steel blade or in a blender. Stir ½ cup of the sugar into chopped cranberries. Cover and allow to stand overnight in the refrigerator. Sift flour with salt, soda, and remaining ¼ cup sugar. Add egg, buttermilk, and melted shortening to flour mixture. Stir by hand until blended; then stir in the cranberries and pecans. Spoon into well greased muffin pans. Bake at 400° for about 20 minutes or until muffins test done. Yield: 18.

Pork Chops with Spicy Tomato Gravy

From "Olympic Celebrations, Southern Living Cooking School" booklet from the Southern Living Cooking School.

Melissa Zinsitz — I've been preparing this dish for several years. It's a crowd pleaser. All my meat-eating friends love it. It's spicy and tasty and calls for convenience foods, which makes it quick and easy.

⅓ cup all-purpose flour
½ teaspoon salt
½ teaspoon ground red pepper, divided
4 (1-inch-thick) lean boneless pork chops
2 tablespoons olive oil, divided
2 garlic cloves, minced divided
4 green onions, finely chopped

1 (1.61-ounce) package fat-free brown-gravy mix (Pioneer recommended)
1 cup reduced-fat milk, divided
1 (14½-ounce) can diced tomatoes, undrained
1 cup water
½ teaspoon dried thyme

Combine flour, salt and ¼ teaspoon red pepper; dredge pork chops in mixture. Heat 1 tablespoon oil in a large nonstick skillet; add pork chops and cook over medium heat until browned on both sides. Remove from skillet and set aside. Add remaining oil to skillet; add garlic and green onions. Cook, stirring constantly, 3 minutes.

Combine gravy mix and ½ cup milk; whisk until blended. Add tomatoes, remaining milk, water, remaining red pepper and thyme to skillet; bring to a boil. Add gravy mixture and stir until smooth, using a wire whisk. Arrange pork chops in skillet, turning to coat with sauce; cover, reduce heat and simmer 15 minutes. Makes 4 servings.

Lemon Bread

½ cup vegetable shortening	¼ teaspoon salt
1 cup sugar	½ cup milk
2 eggs, slightly beaten	½ cup walnuts, finely chopped
1¼ cups plain flour	Grated rind of 1 lemon
1 teaspoon baking powder	

Lemon Sauce:

¼ cup sugar	Juice of 1 large lemon

Preheat oven to 350°. Grease a 5×9-inch loaf pan, and set aside. In an electric mixer, cream the shortening, sugar, and eggs until light and fluffy. Measure flour and sift; then re-measure flour by spooning lightly into a cup. Re-sift flour with baking powder and salt. Beat the dry ingredients into the creamed mixture, alternating with the milk. Stir walnuts and lemon rind in by hand. Pour batter into the loaf pan, and bake in the preheated oven for 45-55 minutes or until loaf tests done. If loaf appears to brown too fast, place a loose sheet of aluminum foil on top of the loaf. Remove loaf from the oven, and pierce the entire surface of the loaf with a cocktail pick. Combine the ingredients of the lemon sauce, and heat to dissolve the sugar; then pour the hot sauce over the hot lemon loaf. Cool bread before cutting into thin slices. Yield: 1 loaf.

Debbie's Sweet Surprise Rolls

1 can Pillsbury's refrigerated crescent rolls	¼ to ½ cup margarine, melted
4 large marshmallows, cut in half	½ cup sugar
	½ teaspoon cinnamon

Preheat oven to 350°. Divide crescent rolls into 8 pieces. Dip each marshmallow half into the melted margarine. Place marshmallow half in the center of the crescent roll dough. Form dough around marshmallow until marshmallow is completely covered. Carefully seal all seams. Mix sugar and cinnamon in a small bowl. Dip rolls into the melted margarine; then roll in the cinnamon sugar mixture. Place in greased muffin pans. Bake in a preheated oven at 350° for 10 minutes or until lightly browned.

Blueberry Muffins

2½ cups plain flour
2½ teaspoons baking powder
⅓ cup sugar
½ teaspoon salt
1 egg yolk, beaten
1 cup milk

4 tablespoons melted margarine
1 egg white, stiffly beaten
1 cup fresh blueberries, washed and drained

Preheat oven to 425°. Measure flour and sift; then re-measure flour by spooning lightly into cup. Re-sift flour with baking powder, sugar, and salt. Combine egg yolk and milk; then add to flour mixture along with the melted margarine. Mix only enough to blend. Fold in stiffly beaten egg white and blueberries until just blended. Spoon into greased muffin pans, and bake at 425° for 25 minutes. Yield: 12 large muffins.

Orange Honey Muffins

1¼ cups plain flour, sifted
½ cup sugar
2 teaspoons baking powder
½ teaspoon salt
¼ cup shortening

2 eggs, well beaten
½ cup milk
Thin orange slices with rind
12 teaspoons honey

Preheat oven to 400°. Sift flour; then re-measure and re-sift with sugar, baking powder, and salt. Blend in shortening; then add eggs and milk. Mix until just moistened. In the bottom of greased muffin tins, place a thin slice of orange and 1 teaspoon of honey. Spoon batter over honey. Bake in a preheated oven at 400° for 18 minutes. Cool 10 minutes; then remove from the muffin tins. Yield: 12 muffins.

Orange Pecan Muffins

1 cup sugar
1 teaspoon grated orange rind
½ cup pecans, chopped
⅓ cup margarine, softened
1 whole egg and 1 egg yolk
2 cups plain flour

2 teaspoons baking powder
½ teaspoon salt
⅔ cup orange juice
18 orange rind slivers, twisted for garnish

Orange Icing:

½ cup powdered sugar
2 to 3 teaspoons orange juice, heated

2 teaspoons margarine, softened

Preheat oven to 375°. In an electric mixer, beat sugar, orange rind, pecans, margarine, egg, and egg yolk for 2 minutes. Measure flour and sift; then re-measure flour by lightly spooning flour into the cup. Sift flour again with the baking powder and salt. Add flour mixture and orange juice; then beat another 2 minutes. Spoon batter into greased muffin pans. Bake in a preheated oven at 375° for about 20 minutes or until muffins test done. Cool muffins before icing. Mix sugar and orange juice into margarine for icing. Ice lightly. Garnish with a twist of orange rind. Yield: 18.

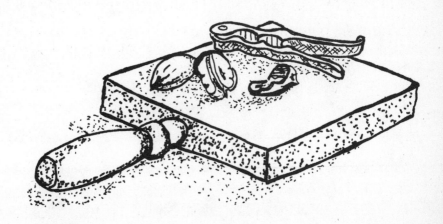

Sour Cream Coffee Cake

1 cup margarine	½ teaspoon vanilla
2 cups sugar	2 cups plain flour
2 eggs	¼ teaspoon salt
1 cup sour cream	1 teaspoon baking powder

Topping:

3 tablespoons brown sugar	2 teaspoons cinnamon
½ cup nuts, chopped	

Preheat oven to 350°. In an electric mixer, cream margarine and sugar; then add eggs, sour cream, and vanilla, and beat on medium speed for 1 minute. Measure flour and sift; then re-measure flour by spooning lightly into cup. Re-sift flour with salt and baking powder; add to the batter. Beat on medium speed for 4 minutes. Pour ½ batter into a greased Bundt pan. Combine all topping ingredients and mix well; then sprinkle ½ topping over the batter. Pour remaining batter into pan and finish with the remaining topping. Bake at 350° for 45 minutes or until cake tests done.

Desserts

Lou's Chocolate Fudge Cake

2 cups plain flour	1 cup water
2 cups sugar	½ cup buttermilk
¼ teaspoon salt	1 teaspoon soda
½ cup margarine	2 eggs, beaten
½ cup vegetable oil	1 teaspoon vanilla
4 tablespoons cocoa	

Frosting:

½ cup margarine	1 pound powdered sugar, sifted
4 tablespoons cocoa	
6 tablespoons milk	⅛ teaspoon salt
	1 teaspoon vanilla

Preheat oven to 350°. Sift flour; then lightly spoon flour into cups to re-measure. Re-sift flour with sugar and salt into an electric mixer bowl. In a saucepan, add margarine, oil, cocoa, and water; bring to a boil. Immediately pour boiling mixture over the flour mixture. Beat on medium speed until well-blended. In a cup, combine buttermilk and soda; then add to the batter. Beat in eggs and vanilla until blended. Grease a deep-lipped 11x16-inch pan (broiler pan). Bake in a preheated oven at 350° for 20 minutes. Frost while still in the pan and hot.

Frosting directions: in a saucepan, bring to a boil margarine, cocoa, and milk. Remove from heat. Beat with the electric mixer while adding sugar, salt, and vanilla. Pour over hot cake, and spread evenly with a broad-blade knife. Cut into squares and serve. Yield: 40-45 squares.

The cake disappears faster than you can believe. Perfect for a charitable bake sale. Just quietly make it while no one is home, lest the bake sale will get only ½ a cake! Wrap each square individually for the sale. There may be only 39 squares instead of the 40 to arrive at the sale, but surely the cake has to be tested first . . . .

Lucy Durr's Coconut Almond Cake

½ cup butter or margarine
2   cups sugar
2½ cups plain flour
2   teaspoons cream of tartar, divided
½ teaspoon soda
½ teaspoon baking powder
¾ cup milk

2   cups fresh coconut, grated very fine or 2 cups frozen coconut, thawed before measuring
2   ounces slivered almonds, chopped fine
½ teaspoon vanilla
8   egg whites, room temperature

Preheat oven to 350°. In an electric mixer, cream butter and sugar. Measure flour, and sift; then re-measure flour by spooning lightly into cups. Re-sift flour with 1 teaspoon of the cream of tartar, soda, and baking powder; add to the creamed mixture along with the milk. Beat on medium speed for 4 minutes. Stir in by hand the coconut, almonds, and vanilla until well-blended. Beat egg whites until very stiff; add remaining 1 teaspoon cream of tartar, and fold into batter. Pour batter into a well-greased tube pan, and bake at 350° for 50-55 minutes.

My grandfather's sister, Lucy Judkins Durr, gave this recipe to him. It had originated on the Judkins Plantation in Wetumpka, Alabama. The recipe probably dates to before The War Between The States.

Chocolate Chip Cake

2	cups plain flour	1	cup sugar
1	teaspoon soda	2	eggs, well-beaten
½	teaspoon salt	8	ounces sour cream
½	cup margarine, softened	2	teaspoons vanilla

Mid-layer and Topping:

1	cup pecans, chopped	6	ounces semi-sweet morsels
½	cup brown sugar		of real chocolate

Preheat oven to 350°. Measure flour and sift; then re-measure flour by spooning lightly into cups. Re-sift flour with soda and salt; set aside. Grease a Bundt pan very generously with shortening. In an electric mixer, cream the margarine and sugar until light and fluffy. Then add eggs, sour cream, and vanilla; beat at medium speed for 2 minutes. Slowly add the flour mixture and beat for 4 minutes. In a small bowl, combine pecans, brown sugar, and chocolate morsels; toss to mix. Pour ½ batter into the greased pan, and sprinkle with ½ the pecan mixture. Pour other ½ batter over the pecan mixture, and sprinkle with remaining topping. Bake in the preheated oven at 350° for 35 minutes or until cake tests done. Let cake cool in the pan for 30 minutes; then turn out onto a cake stand. Carefully turn cake over to show the decorative topping.

This cake needs no frosting since it is quite rich with chocolate and pecans.

Dorothy's Coconut Sour Cream Cake

The recipe requires the cake to be refrigerated for 3 days before serving.

1   **Duncan Hines Butter Recipe
    Golden Cake Mix**

Filling and Icing:
16 **ounces sour cream**
2   **cups sugar**
12 to 14 **ounces frozen coconut,
    divided**

4   **ounces whipped topping,
    thawed**

Make cake as directed on the box for layer cakes. Cool cakes; then slice horizontally. Make filling by mixing sour cream, sugar, and 10 ounces of the coconut. Reserve ½ cup filling to use in icing. Spoon filling in a thick layer between each cake layer, allowing it to run down the sides. For the top of the cake, mix whipped topping with the reserved ½ cup filling and ice the cake. At the end of the 3 days, sprinkle remaining coconut over the top, sides, and base of the cake since the filling runs and will need a touch up before serving.

The suspenseful wait only enhances this superb cake!

Orange Butter Frosting

6   **tablespoons margarine,
    softened**
3   **cups powdered sugar, sifted**
1½ **tablespoons white Karo
    syrup**

3   **tablespoons orange juice**
1½ **teaspoons orange peel,
    grated**

In an electric mixer, cream margarine and sugar until fluffy. Add Karo, orange juice, and orange peel. Beat until smooth. Yield: frosting for a 2 layer cake or 48 cup cakes.

Lemon Buttermilk Cake

3 cups plain flour	1 cup vegetable oil
½ teaspoon salt	4 eggs
½ teaspoon soda	1 cup buttermilk
½ teaspoon baking powder	2 tablespoons lemon extract
2 cups sugar	

Glaze:

2½ cups powdered sugar, sifted	5 tablespoons orange juice
5 tablespoons lemon juice	½ teaspoon salt

Preheat oven to 325°. Measure flour and sift; then re-measure flour by lightly spooning into cups. Re-sift flour with salt, soda, and baking powder; set aside. In an electric mixer on low speed, beat sugar, oil, eggs, buttermilk, and extract until just blended. Add the flour mixture to the egg mixture slowly while blending; then beat on medium speed for 4 minutes. Pour batter into a greased and floured tube pan. Bake in a preheated oven at 325° for 1 hour or until cake tests done. Mix all glaze ingredients and set aside. When cake is done, remove from the oven, and loosen the edges while cake is hot and still in the pan. Pour glaze over the hot cake. Return cake to the oven for 3 minutes. Remove cake from the oven after the 3 minutes, and allow to cool in the pan, and the glaze to set before turning cake out of pan.

Lemon Buttercream Frosting

¼ cup margarine, softened	2 tablespoons lemon juice
1 pound powdered sugar, sifted	1 tablespoon grated lemon peel
4-5 tablespoons Half and Half	

In an electric mixer, cream margarine and sugar until fluffy. Add Half and Half, lemon juice, and lemon peel; beat until smooth. Yield: frosting for a 3 layer cake.

Strawberry Tall Cake

1	package Pillsbury yellow cake mix with pudding	8	ounces cream cheese, softened
2	pints fresh strawberries, (reserve 5 whole strawberries)	½	cup granulated sugar
		12	ounces whipped topping, thawed
1	(16-ounce) jar strawberry glaze	1	cup powdered sugar

Bake cake according to package instructions for 2 layer cakes; cool completely. Slice the layers in half, and place in the freezer. Slice strawberries, and mix with the strawberry glaze. Reserve 3 tablespoons of the mixture for the top of the cake. In an electric mixer, beat cream cheese, granulated sugar, whipped topping, and powdered sugar until well-blended. On a serving platter or cake stand, place a halved layer of the frozen cake. Spread a thin coating of the cream cheese mixture on the layer; then cover with ⅓ of the glaze mixture. Repeat process with 2 more frozen halved layers. Place the remaining frozen halved layer on top, and cover top of the cake with the cream cheese mixture. Place the reserved 3 tablespoons of glaze mixture in the center of the cake and decorate with the reserved whole strawberries. Refrigerate the cake until serving time.

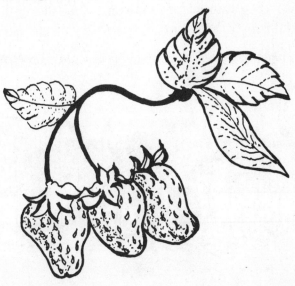

English Rum Cake

1   cup granulated sugar,
    divided
5   eggs, separated and room
    temperature
Grated rind of ½ lemon
1   cup plain flour

Pinch of salt
4   tablespoons margarine
½   cup powdered sugar
3   tablespoons rum
Sweetened whipped cream,
    optional

Preheat oven to 350°. Grease a Bundt pan and set aside. Caster the sugar by placing sugar in a food processor with a steel blade or in a blender. Run on high speed for 4 minutes to make the sugar finer, but not powdered. In an electric mixer, beat egg yolks, ¼ cup of the sugar, and lemon rind for 4 minutes on medium speed. Sift flour with the salt and set aside. In the electric mixer with clean beaters (do not allow any yolk to get into whites), beat room temperature egg whites until soft peaks form. Gradually add the remaining ¾ cup sugar, and beat until stiff peaks form. Lightly fold flour mixture into the yolks; then fold in whites. Pour batter into the greased Bundt pan, and place in the center of the preheated oven without a rack overhead (cake needs "headroom"). Bake at 350° for 50 minutes or until cake tests done. Cool for 20 minutes before turning out of the pan. Melt the margarine; stir in powdered sugar and rum. Pour glaze over the cake when it is cold. Cover cake with whipped cream before slicing. Refrigerate any unused portion.

Very, very light cake with a "rummy" flavor. Delightful, different, and so British.

Cranberry Nut Cake

2¼ cups plain flour
1 cup sugar
1 teaspoon baking powder
1 teaspoon soda
¼ teaspoon salt
1 cup nuts, chopped

1¼ cups fresh cranberries, chopped (use food processor or blender)
2 tablespoons orange juice
2 eggs, beaten
¾ cup vegetable oil
1 cup buttermilk

Preheat oven to 350°. Measure flour and sift; then re-measure flour by lightly spooning into cups. In a large bowl, re-sift flour with sugar, baking powder, soda, and salt. Stir in the nuts, cranberries, and orange juice. Mix together the eggs, oil, and buttermilk until well-blended; then stir into the dry ingredients. Mix thoroughly. Grease and flour a Bundt pan, (flouring is essential for this cake). Pour batter into the pan, and bake in the preheated oven at 350° for 45 to 50 minutes or until cake tests done. Allow cake to cool for 30 minutes before turning out of pan. Completely cool cake; then wrap in plastic wrap and foil, and refrigerate. This cake also freezes very well.

Nobby Apple Cake

3 tablespoons margarine
1 cup sugar
1 egg, beaten
1 cup plain flour, sifted
1 teaspoon baking powder
½ teaspoon cinnamon

½ teaspoon nutmeg
½ teaspoon salt
3 cups apples, peeled and diced
¼ cup pecans, chopped
1 teaspoon vanilla

Preheat oven to 350°. In an electric mixer, cream margarine, sugar, and egg for about 2 minutes or until well-mixed and light. Sift together flour, baking powder, cinnamon, nutmeg, and salt. Add the flour mixture to the creamed mixture slowly, and beat until well-blended. By hand, stir in apples, pecans, and vanilla. Pour into a greased 8x8 inch square baking dish. Bake at 350° for 40-45 minutes. Serve this cake hot or cold. It is good topped with either ice cream or whipped cream. Serves 8-9.

Mary's Mississippi Mud Cake

1	cup margarine	1½	cups plain flour
2	cups sugar	¼	teaspoon salt
½	cup cocoa	1	cup pecans, chopped
4	eggs, beaten	6½	ounces miniature
1	teaspoon vanilla		marshmallows

Chocolate Frosting:

½	cup margarine, melted	½	teaspoon vanilla
½	cup milk	1	pound powdered sugar,
¼	teaspoon salt		sifted
		⅓	cup cocoa

Preheat oven to 350°. In an electric mixer, cream margarine, sugar, and cocoa; then add eggs and vanilla. Beat for 1 minute on medium speed. Measure flour and sift; then re-measure flour by spooning lightly into cup. Re-sift flour with salt, and beat into batter for 4 minutes on medium speed. Add the pecans and stir by hand. Bake in a greased 9x13 inch baking pan at 350° for 35 minutes. Remove cake from oven, and pour marshmallows over the top; then return cake to oven just long enough to soften the marshmallows. Remove from oven, and immediately pour icing over the softened marshmallows. With a broad-blade knife, swirl icing and marshmallows together into a "rocky road" effect. Additional pecans can be sprinkled over top, if desired. Let cake cool before cutting into squares. Yield: 16-20.

Chocolate Frosting:

In an electric mixer, combine melted margarine, milk, salt, and vanilla. Beat on low speed until blended; then beat in powdered sugar and cocoa until smooth.

Joe's Sponge Cake (Non-edible)

2	pieces foam rubber, 10-inches square each	1	aerosol can cake decorating frosting
1	band saw	1	large can chocolate frosting
			Lots of nerve

Using the band saw, cut a 9-inch round from each piece of foam. Ice first piece of foam, and place on a silver cake stand; then ice the remaining piece of foam, and place it on top of first "layer". Ice sides to completely conceal the foam. Decorate top with aerosol frosting.

This makes a beautiful cake. I suggest you have a real one in reserve to prevent mutiny!

Applesauce Cakes

Makes 3 loaf cakes.

4	cups sugar	2	teaspoons nutmeg
1	cup vegetable shortening	2	teaspoons salt
4	eggs, beaten	2	teaspoons ground cloves
8	cups plain flour	4	cups applesauce
4	teaspoons cinnamon	7½	ounces raisins
4	teaspoons soda	2	cups pecans, chopped

Preheat oven to 300°. In an electric mixer, cream sugar and shortening until light and fluffy; then add eggs, and beat 3 minutes. Measure flour and sift; then re-measure flour by spooning lightly into cup. Re-sift flour with cinnamon, soda, nutmeg, salt, and cloves. Add flour mixture to batter alternately with applesauce, raisins, and nuts. Mix well on low speed. Pour into 3 greased loaf pans, and bake at 300° for 1½ to 2 hours. After 1½ hours, begin testing for doneness.

These cakes were always made at my grandmother's home at Christmas. They make beautiful gifts, anytime, when wrapped tightly with plastic and tied with a bright bit of yarn and a sprig of greenery.

Lemon Cheese Pound Cake

½ cup vegetable shortening	6 eggs, room temperature
½ cup margarine, softened	4 teaspoons lemon juice
8 ounces cream cheese, softened	2 cups plain flour
	1 cup self-rising flour
3 cups sugar	

Frosting:

1 pound powdered sugar, sifted	Small amount of milk to thin frosting, if needed
8 ounces cream cheese, softened	
1½ teaspoons lemon juice	

Start cake in a **cold** oven. In an electric mixer, cream shortening, margarine, and cream cheese. Add sugar, and beat until fluffy. Add eggs, one at a time, and beat well; then add lemon juice. Measure both flours and sift; then re-measure by lightly spooning into cups. Add flour slowly to the batter, and beat on medium speed for 4 minutes. Pour into a greased and floured tube pan. Place in a cold oven; then turn baking temperature to 275°. Bake 1 hour and 30 to 40 minutes. Do not open oven door while cake is baking. When cooking time is completed, remove cake and cool for 10 minutes before turning out of pan. To frost, beat in an electric mixer the sugar, cream cheese, and lemon juice. Add milk to thin, if needed. Frost cake when cooled.

Nutty Chocolate Cola Cake

2	cups plain flour	1	teaspoon soda
2	cups granulated sugar	2	eggs
½	cup margarine	1½	cups miniature
½	cup solid shortening		marshmallows
3	tablespoons cocoa	1	teaspoon vanilla
1	cup cola	½	teaspoon salt
½	cup buttermilk		

Frosting:

½	cup margarine	1	teaspoon vanilla
2	tablespoons cocoa	1	cup nuts, chopped
6	tablespoons cola	¼	teaspoon salt
1	(1-pound) box powdered sugar, sifted		

Preheat oven to 350°. Measure flour and sift; then re-measure flour by spooning lightly into cup. Re-sift flour with sugar into an electric mixer bowl, and set aside. In a saucepan, melt margarine and shortening; stir in cocoa and cola. Bring to a rapid boil; pour into the flour mixture. Beat on medium speed with an electric mixer until well-blended. Add buttermilk, soda, eggs, marshmallows, vanilla, and salt. Beat for 2 minutes. Pour into a greased 9x13 inch baking dish. Bake in a preheated oven at 350° for 45 minutes. Frost cake immediately after removing from the oven, while still in the baking dish.

Frosting:

In a saucepan, bring margarine, cocoa, and cola to a boil; add powdered sugar, vanilla, nuts, and salt. Mix well, and pour hot frosting over the hot cake in the baking dish. Cool and cut into small squares.

Tipsy Pecan Cake

1 cup margarine, softened	1 cup bourbon
2 cups sugar	4 cups pecans, chopped
6 eggs, separated	coarsely
4 cups plain flour, divided	8 ounces chopped candied
Pinch of nutmeg	cherries
2 teaspoons baking powder	

Preheat oven to 325°. In an electric mixer, cream margarine and sugar until very light and fluffy. Add egg yolks, one at a time. Beat for 3 minutes on medium speed. Measure 3¾ cups flour and sift; then re-measure flour by spooning lightly into cup. Re-sift flour with nutmeg and baking powder. Add flour mixture to the creamed mixture alternately with the bourbon until well blended. In a small bowl, combine remaining ¼ cup flour with pecans and cherries. Toss fruit and nuts to coat with the flour. By hand, stir the fruit and nut mixture into the batter; mix well. Using the electric mixer with a fresh bowl and beaters, beat egg whites until stiff, but not dry. Fold egg whites gently into the batter. Pour into a greased and floured 10-inch Bundt pan. Bake in a preheated oven at 325° for about 1 hour and 40 minutes or until cake tests done. If cake should brown on top too quickly, cover with a loose sheet of aluminum foil.

Yellow Layer Cake

1½ cups sugar	2 teaspoons baking powder
1 cup margarine, softened	1 cup milk
4 eggs, room temperature	1 teaspoon vanilla
4 cups plain flour	

Preheat oven to 325°. In an electric mixer, cream sugar and margarine. Add eggs, one at a time, beating well. In a separate bowl, sift flour; then re-measure by lightly spooning flour into cups, and re-sift with baking powder. Add the milk, and the flour mixture alternately to the creamed mixture. Mix for 2 minutes on medium speed. Add vanilla, and mix until just blended. Bake in 3 greased 8-inch layer pans at 325° for 25 to 30 minutes, or until cakes test done. Allow layers to cool completely before frosting with chocolate frosting.

Chocolate Frosting

½ cup margarine
4 tablespoons cocoa
6 tablespoons milk
1 teaspoon vanilla

¼ teaspoon salt
1 pound powdered sugar,
   sifted
1 cup nuts, chopped

In a heavy saucepan, bring margarine, cocoa, and milk to a boil; add vanilla, salt, and sugar. Remove from heat, and beat until creamy; stir in nuts, and beat to coat the nuts. Frosting will cover a 3 layer cake.

Julia Mae's Poppy Seed Cake

1 box white cake mix
1 cup hot water
4 eggs
½ cup oil

1 (3½-ounce) box instant
   toasted coconut pudding mix
¼ cup poppy seeds

Preheat oven to 350°. Beat all ingredients in an electric mixer for 4 minutes. Pour batter into a well-greased tube pan. Bake at 350° for 40 minutes or until cake tests done. Cool in the pan for 20 minutes before turning out. Cake can be served plain or with a frosting or glaze.

Island Rum Cakes

1 loaf angel food cake
¾ cup margarine, melted
1 egg white
3 tablespoons rum

1 (1 pound) box powdered
   sugar
2 cups pecans, finely chopped

Cut the entire angel food loaf into 1-inch cubes. Melt margarine, and allow to cool; stir in the egg white (unbeaten) and rum. Beat in powdered sugar to make a soft frosting. Frost all sides of cake cubes; then roll cubes in the chopped pecans to coat. Freeze or refrigerate cakes until ready to serve.

Cookies

Rosettes or The Archbishop's Temptation

The most essential ingredients for this recipe are patience and a very good friend. Set aside a sunny day (never make these on a rainy day), and invite a "Rosette-loving" friend to help, and split the rewards. Items needed other than the batter ingredients are:

Plenty of absorbent paper towels
As many cookie sheets as you and your friend have
2 (48-ounce) bottles Wesson oil
2 (1-pound) boxes powdered sugar
Plenty of gallon-size Ziploc bags
1 large electric skillet
A single or double Rosette iron made of **cast** aluminum (light weight, less expensive versions do not work well)
O.K.—you're ready to begin. Make 2 or 3 separate batches of the Rosette batter, and pour into 2 (8-inch) pie dishes, and refrigerate for at least 30 minutes. Fill electric skillet ¾ full of oil, and heat to 400° exactly. Place Rosette iron into the heating oil and prop securely if the iron does not stand alone. It is essential to keep the iron's Rosette form in the 400° oil at all times.

2 eggs	2 teaspoons sugar
1 cup milk	1 cup plain flour, sifted
½ teaspoon salt	

Place all ingredients in a food processor or blender, and mix until well blended. Make another whole separate batch of batter; then refrigerate as instructed above. When both batters have chilled for at least 30 minutes, remove one pie dish from refrigerator, and beat with a fork for a few seconds. The batter should be the consistency of heavy cream. Keep batter at that consistency throughout the cooking time (a very small amount of milk may be needed to thin batter later). Remove hot Rosette form from hot oil, and shake excess oil, **very carefully,** back into the skillet; then immediately dip form into batter to no more than ¾ the depth of the Rosette form. Immediately return form with batter on it to oil. Allow the batter to fry on the form for a few seconds; then carefully and gently shake form, in the oil, to float the Rosette free. Allow Rosette to brown **lightly;** then turn to brown other side with a long-handle two-prong fork. Lift Rosette; gently and carefully shake off excess oil. Drain on paper towel in a single layer only. Do **not** stack. Form a

working pattern with your friend—one forms the Rosettes, and the other cooks and drains. The first few Rosettes are usually not well formed. Do not despair! Beat batter to blend in the oil added by the form. Continue making until all the batter is used; then start on the other dish of batter. Two batches will make a great number of Rosettes. Three batches will make a mountain, for gift-giving. When all Rosettes are made and cooled, stack 5 at a time in a bowl, and sift powdered sugar over each Rosette. Place gently into Ziploc bags and seal. Rosettes freeze very well and require no thawing time. More powdered sugar may be added after freezing to make the Rosettes pretty. If not frozen, seal in air-tight containers. Hopefully, these very explicit directions will give you "instant experience."

At the after-rehearsal party of a mutual relative, temptation, in the form of Rosettes, hit, at that time Monsignor, and now Archbishop Oscar Lipscomb of Mobile, Alabama. Try as he may, the "powdered sugar evidence" stayed with his black suit. As I recall, he did leave that evening with a smile on his face.

Pecan Snowballs

1   cup margarine, softened
¼   cup sugar
1   cup ground pecans

2   cups plain flour
Powdered sugar, sifted

Preheat oven to 300°. In an electric mixer, cream margarine and sugar. Add pecans and flour; mix well. Shape the dough into small balls. Place the balls on an ungreased cookie sheet, and bake at 300° for about 35-45 minutes or until lightly browned. Remove from oven, and immediately roll in powdered sugar. Allow to cool; then roll in powdered sugar again. Yield: 98.

Nanaimo Bars

¾ cup margarine plus 1
    tablespoon, divided
¼ cup granulated sugar
5 tablespoons cocoa
2 eggs
1 teaspoon vanilla

1⅔ cups fine graham cracker
    crumbs
1 cup frozen, flaked coconut
½ cup nuts, chopped
2 cups powdered sugar, sifted
4 squares semisweet chocolate

Grease a 9 inch square baking dish, and set aside. In a saucepan, cook until blended ½ cup of the margarine, granulated sugar and cocoa. Cool chocolate mixture; then beat in 1 egg and vanilla. Cook over medium heat until smooth and slightly thickened. Stir in the graham cracker crumbs, coconut, and nuts; mix well. Press mixture into the greased dish. In an electric mixer, cream ¼ cup of the margarine, powdered sugar, and remaining egg. Spread over the crumb mixture in the dish, and chill in the refrigerator for about 15 minutes. In a double boiler over hot water, melt chocolate with remaining 1 tablespoon margarine. Spread over the creamed layer, and refrigerate until well set. Cut into small squares.

Named for a city on the southern end of Vancouver Island, British Colum-bia. It is an Indian word pronounced "nah NI moh", meaning home of five bands.

Sweet Kisses

½ cup margarine, softened
½ cup sugar
1 teaspoon vanilla
2 cups plain flour

1 large package kisses or
    silver bells, (remove all of
    the foil from candies)
Powdered sugar

Preheat oven to 375°. In an electric mixer, cream margarine, sugar, and vanilla. Sift flour over creamed mixture; then mix into a dough. Pinch off pieces of dough, roll into a ball, then flatten. Place a kiss that has had silver foil removed, in the center, and wrap dough around the candy. Bake on an ungreased cookie sheet at 375° for about 6 minutes. When cool, roll in powdered sugar. These cookies freeze well.

Tea Cakes

½	cup margarine	2	tablespoons milk
1	cup sugar	1	teaspoon baking powder
⅛	teaspoon salt	1	teaspoon vanilla
2	eggs	3	cups plain flour, sifted

Preheat oven to 325°. In an electric mixer, cream margarine and sugar; add salt. Beat in eggs one at a time; then add milk, baking powder, and vanilla. Mix until well-blended. Slowly add the sifted flour to form a soft dough. Refrigerate dough for 2 hours. Divide dough into 3 pieces for easier handling. On a floured surface, roll dough with a floured rolling pin **very** thin; then cut out with a cookie cutter. Place cookies on a greased cookie sheet, and bake in a preheated oven at 325° for about 10 minutes or until very light brown. Watch the cookies carefully since they are thin and some brown quicker than others.

Everyone seems to remember having their grandmother serve Tea Cakes. My husband's mother made them for a friend from Finland. He was amazed—they tasted just like the ones his grandmother used to make!

Oatmeal Cookies

1	cup granulated sugar	1½	cups plain flour, sifted
1	cup packed brown sugar	1	teaspoon soda
1	cup shortening	½	teaspoon salt
2	eggs	1	cup raisins
1	teaspoon vanilla	1	cup pecans, chopped
3	cups quick oats		

Preheat oven to 375°. In an electric mixer, cream both sugars and shortening until light. Add eggs and vanilla; beat until fluffy. Stir oats into mixture. Re-measure sifted flour by spooning lightly into cup. Re-sift flour with soda and salt. Add flour mixture to the batter and mix well. By hand, stir in raisins and pecans; blend well. Shape dough into small balls, and place on greased cookie sheets. Bake in a preheated 375° oven for 10 to 15 minutes. Cool slightly before removing from cookie sheets. Yield: about 6 dozen.

Chocolate Mint Triple-Decker Brownies

Brownie:

½ cup cocoa	2 eggs
½ teaspoon soda	1⅓ cups plain flour, unsifted
⅔ cup vegetable oil, divided	1 teaspoon vanilla
½ cup boiling water	¼ teaspoon salt
2 cups sugar	

Frosting:

2 cups powdered sugar, sifted	½ teaspoon peppermint extract
½ cup margarine, softened	Green food color
2 tablespoons milk	

Glaze:

6 ounces semisweet chocolate morsels	6 tablespoons margarine

Preheat oven to 350°. To prepare brownies, use an electric mixer, and combine cocoa, soda, and ⅓ cup of the vegetable oil. Add the boiling water; stir until mixture thickens. Mix in sugar, eggs, and remaining oil until smooth. Slowly add flour, vanilla, and salt; blend completely. Pour into greased 9x13-inch baking pan. Bake at 350° for 35-40 minutes. Cool completely before frosting. Do not remove from pan.

Frosting is prepared by creaming powdered sugar with margarine; then add milk and peppermint, and beat until light and fluffy. Add green food color to desired tint. Spread the frosting over cooled brownies, and set aside.

For the glaze, melt semisweet morsels and margarine in a double boiler over simmering water. Pour over frosted brownies, and allow to harden at room temperature. If in a hurry, brownies can be refrigerated to speed the setting process. Cut into 1½-inch squares. Yield: 32.

Mexican Wedding Cookies

1 cup margarine
⅓ cup granulated sugar
Scant ⅛ teaspoon salt
2 cups plain flour

1½ teaspoons vanilla
1 cup pecans or walnuts, chopped
Powdered sugar

Preheat oven to 300°. In a saucepan, melt margarine; then add granulated sugar, salt, and flour. Remove from heat and stir to blend. Add vanilla and nuts; mix well. Form cookies as small balls or in crescents. Bake on an ungreased cookie sheet in a preheated oven at 300° for 25 to 30 minutes. Do not brown. Remove from cookie sheet, and carefully roll hot cookies in powdered sugar. Yield: 4 dozen.

Old favorites are hard to beat, and these definitely are favorites. Sometimes called Sand Tarts or Crescents, they're delightful, delicate cookies with a large "fan club."

Sour Cream Cookies

These cookies can be made plain or the dough divided into 4 portions, and extra ingredients added to make a variety of cookies.

Basic recipe:
1 cup vegetable shortening
1 cup sugar
2 egg yolks, beaten
½ cup sour cream

1 teaspoon vanilla
4 cups plain flour
½ teaspoon salt
½ teaspoon soda

Extra ingredients:
Make one batch plain, one with 1 cup chopped nuts, one with 1 cup frozen coconut, and one with ⅓ cup cocoa.

Preheat oven to 375°. In an electric mixer, cream the vegetable shortening and sugar; then add egg yolks, sour cream, and vanilla. Sift together the flour, salt, and soda; add to the dough, and mix well. Divide dough into 4 portions, if using the variations, and mix in one extra ingredient to each portion. Roll a teaspoonful into a ball; then flatten with a fork. Place on a greased cookie sheet. Bake at 375° for 10 to 12 minutes. Yield: 5 dozen.

Chocolate Frills

3   tablespoons shortening
2   squares unsweetened
     chocolate
1   cup sugar
2   eggs
1   teaspoon vanilla

1   cup flour, sifted
1¼ teaspoons baking powder
Pinch of salt
½   cup nuts, chopped (optional)
Powdered sugar

Preheat oven to 325°. In a saucepan, melt shortening and chocolate; remove from the heat. Add sugar, and beat well. Add eggs, one at a time, and continue to beat until mixed. Stir in vanilla, flour, baking powder, salt, and nuts; mix well. Place batter into the refrigerator until well chilled. Form into tiny balls, and roll in powdered sugar. Place balls on a greased cookie sheet. Bake in a preheated oven at 325° for 10 to 12 minutes. Take cookies from the oven, and immediately remove from the cookie sheet. Yield: 50-60 cookies.

Stay Up All Night Cookies

Make when cookies can remain in the oven overnight, and it is not raining.

2   egg whites, room
     temperature
Scant ⅛ teaspoon salt
⅔   cup sugar

½   teaspoon vanilla
6   ounces semisweet real
     chocolate morsels
1   cup pecans, chopped

Preheat oven to 375°. In an electric mixer, beat egg whites that are room temperature to soft peaks; then gradually add salt, sugar, and vanilla. Beat until stiff peaks form. Carefully fold in the semisweet morsels and pecans. Grease a cookie sheet and drop cookies by teaspoonsful. Place the cookie sheet into the preheated oven; then immediately turn oven off. Do not open door of oven until removing cookies in the morning. If it's not convenient to leave cookies in the oven overnight, allow them to stay in the cooling oven for several hours. Store in an airtight container; moisture from the air will cause them to become sticky.

These cookies are a crunch of "air" flavored with chocolate and pecans.

Elise's Paper Thin Cookies

½   cup margarine, softened
1   cup sugar
1   egg
½   teaspoon baking powder
¼   teaspoon cream of tartar

1½ cups plain flour, unsifted
1   teaspoon vanilla
½   teaspoon cinnamon
2   teaspoons sugar

Preheat oven to 350°. In an electric mixer, cream margarine and 1 cup sugar. Add egg, and beat for 1 minute. Beat in baking powder, cream of tartar, flour, and vanilla until well-blended. Refrigerate batter for ½ hour for easier handling; then form batter into small balls. Place the balls into the freezer for ½ hour for easier handling. Remove a few balls at a time from freezer, and flatten with the heel of the hand onto a cookie sheet sprayed with vegetable oil. Make the cookies as flat as possible. Mix cinnamon and 2 teaspoons sugar in a small bowl and lightly sprinkle each cookie. Bake in a preheated oven at 350° for about 5 minutes until lightly browned. Watch extremely carefully since cookies are very thin and bake quickly. Remove cookies from cookie sheets immediately after taking out of oven. Do not stack. Allow cookies to completely cool before storing. Yield: 45-50.

These cookies are so deliciously thin and crisp. Double the recipe, and keep baked cookies in a container in the freezer. They don't require more than a few minutes to thaw before serving. The cookie batter can be made ahead of baking time and stored in the refrigerator for as long as a week.

Ice Box Cookies

½ cup margarine, softened
2 cups brown sugar
2 eggs
3½ cups flour

1 teaspoon soda
½ teaspoon salt
1 cup nuts, chopped

Preheat oven to 375° about 15 minutes before baking time. In an electric mixer, cream margarine and brown sugar. Add eggs, and beat well. Measure flour, and sift; then re-measure flour by lightly spooning into cup. Re-sift flour, soda, and salt. Mix flour mixture into creamed mixture, and beat for 1 minute. By hand, stir in the nuts until well-blended. Place batter into the refrigerator to chill. When chilled, form batter into rolls the size of a silver dollar. Wrap in plastic, and freeze. At baking time, slice frozen dough thin and place on a greased cookie sheet. Bake in a preheated oven at 375° for about 6 minutes. Watch carefully; cookies are thin and bake quickly.

Nothing new about this one—was made in my husband's grandmother's home and handed down to his mother and aunt, Helen. It's still a family favorite. Some things don't change—fortunately.

Nancy's Lemon Yummies

1 cup margarine
½ cup powdered sugar
2¼ cups plain flour, divided
2 cups granulated sugar

4 eggs, well beaten
6 tablespoons lemon juice
Extra powdered sugar for
   decoration

Preheat oven to 350°. In an electric mixer, cream margarine, powdered sugar, and 2 cups of the flour into a dough. In a greased 2-quart baking dish, pat the dough into an even layer. Bake at 350° for 25 minutes. Mix granulated sugar, eggs, lemon juice, and the remaining ¼ cup of flour until well-blended. Pour egg mixture over the hot crust, and bake at 350° for 30 minutes. Cool completely. Dust with a light layer of powdered sugar, and cut into small squares. Refrigerate after 2 hours. Yield: 24.

Southland Layer Bars

½ cup margarine, melted
1 cup graham cracker crumbs
1 cup frozen coconut, thawed
14 ounces sweetened condensed milk
6 ounces semisweet chocolate morsels
1 cup pecans, chopped

Layer ingredients in a 9×13-inch pan: melted margarine, graham cracker crumbs, coconut, condensed milk, semisweet morsels, and pecans. Bake at 350° for 25-30 minutes. Cool before cutting into bars. Yield: 36.

Christmas Fruit and Nut Cookies

1 cup margarine
1½ cups sugar
3 eggs, separated and room temperature
3½ cups plain flour, divided
1 pound candied cherries, chopped
1 pound candied pineapple, chopped
2 cups golden raisins
2 cups pecans, chopped
1 teaspoon soda
½ teaspoon salt
1 teaspoon vanilla
2 tablespoons bourbon or rum

Preheat oven to 350°. Cream margarine and sugar in an electric mixer; then add egg yolks, and mix well. Sprinkle enough of the flour over the chopped fruit, raisins, and pecans to coat. Sift together remaining flour, soda, and salt. Combine creamed mixture and flour mixture; blend well. Add vanilla, bourbon, and stir in the fruit mixture; blend. Beat egg whites until stiff, and fold in. Drop by teaspoonsful on a greased cookie sheet, and bake in a preheated oven at 350° for 10-15 minutes. Yield: 150 cookies.

This batter can be prepared several weeks ahead and frozen until needed. The cookies also freeze very well after baking.

Christmas Cherry Cheesecake Squares

⅓ cup margarine, cut into
chunks
⅓ cup firmly packed brown
sugar
1 cup plain flour
¼ cup granulated sugar
8 ounces cream cheese,
softened

1 egg
1 tablespoon lemon juice
¼ cup glazed green cherries,
chopped
¼ cup glazed red cherries,
chopped
½ cup pecans, chopped

Preheat oven to 350°. In a food processor using the steel blade, place the margarine, brown sugar, and flour; blend into crumbs. Reserve ½ cup of this mixture for topping. Press remaining mixture into an 8-inch square greased baking dish. Bake at 350° for 10-12 minutes. In an electric mixer, cream the granulated sugar and cream cheese; then add egg and lemon juice. Beat on medium speed for 1-2 minutes; stir in both kinds of cherries and the pecans. Spread the cherry mixture over the crust, and sprinkle top with remaining crumb mixture. Bake at 350° for 20 minutes or until filling is set, and the top is lightly browned. Cool and cut into squares. Refrigerate to store. Yield: 12-16 large squares.

Pies

Black Bottom Pie

Make early in the day to allow time to set up. Do not make the day before serving. This recipe makes 2 pies.

1 envelope plain gelatin
¼ cup cold water
1 cup sugar, divided
½ teaspoon salt
4 tablespoons cornstarch
2 cups milk
4 eggs, separated
6 ounces semisweet real chocolate morsels, reserve enough to make Chocolate Leaves (see A Duke's Mixture)

1 teaspoon vanilla
2 baked and cooled 8-inch pie crusts
1 tablespoon rum, bourbon, sherry, or rum extract
¼ teaspoon cream of tartar
½ pint whipping cream

Pour gelatin into the cold water and set aside. In a saucepan, combine ½ cup of the sugar with salt and cornstarch; stir in milk. Cook over low heat, stirring constantly, until thickened. Beat egg yolks in a small bowl; then **slowly** add a **small** amount of hot mixture into the eggs to bring egg yolks to cooking temperature. Add egg yolk mixture to sugar mixture slowly, and cook, stirring for 2 minutes. Remove from heat. Pour semisweet morsels into a bowl, and add 1½ cups of hot mixture. Stir until chocolate is melted. Add vanilla, and pour mixture into each cooled pie crust, dividing evenly. Place pie crusts in refrigerator to cool. Return to remaining mixture in saucepan, and add gelatin; mix very carefully, and cool to lukewarm. Stir in the rum. In an electric mixer, beat egg whites until stiff; then add cream of tartar and remaining ½ cup sugar. Fold egg whites into the rum-flavored custard, and pour over the chilled chocolate custard in pie crusts; chill. Whip cream, and sweeten to taste. Spread whipped cream over custard after it has set up in the refrigerator. Decorate the top of the pies with the Chocolate Leaves. Keep pies refrigerated. Yield: 2 pies.

Rich, but very light and so beautiful. Definitely on the top of the "favorites' list" at our house.

Lisa's Imperial Apple Pie

1 cup brown sugar
2 tablespoons flour
¼ teaspoon cinnamon
1 tablespoon lemon juice

4 large green apples, peeled and sliced
1 unbaked 9-inch pie shell

Topping:
¾ cup brown sugar
¼ teaspoon nutmeg

1 cup plain flour
½ cup margarine, melted

Preheat oven to 350°. Mix together brown sugar, flour, and cinnamon. Pour lemon juice over apples; then stir together the apples, and the sugar mixture. Place in unbaked pie shell. Mix together all topping ingredients until well-blended; then press evenly with a fork over top of the apples in the pie shell. Bake in the preheated oven for 45 minutes.

Not the typical apple pie. It is tart, with a tantalizingly crisp topping.

Pecan Pie

1 cup sugar
½ cup corn syrup
¼ cup margarine, melted

3 eggs, well beaten
1 cup pecans, halved
1 unbaked pie crust

Combine sugar, syrup, and margarine; beat until well-blended. Add beaten eggs, and mix thoroughly. Stir in the pecans; then pour into the unbaked pie crust. Bake at 350° for 40 to 45 minutes or until pie is set. Serve hot or cold.

Heavenly Chocolate Cheese Pie

Make pie one day before serving.

6   ounces semisweet real
    chocolate morsels, reserve 2
    dozen for garnish
6   ounces cream cheese,
    softened
¾   cup sugar, divided
1   teaspoon vanilla

2   eggs, separated and room
    temperature
1   cup whipping cream, divided
1   graham cracker pie crust

Melt chocolate in a double boiler over hot, not boiling, water. Do not allow chocolate to cook, just melt. Combine softened cream cheese, ½ cup of the sugar, vanilla, and beaten egg yolks. Slowly, stir the melted chocolate into the cream cheese mixture. Allow to cool. Whip the cream, reserving ½ cup, and add to chocolate mixture. Beat egg whites to soft peaks; then gradually add remaining ¼ cup sugar and beat to stiff peaks. Fold egg whites into chocolate mixture. Pour into pie crust, top with reserved whipped cream, and dot with chocolate morsels. Freeze overnight. Remove from freezer about 5 minutes before serving. Very rich, slice accordingly. Serves 8.

True chocolate decadence, and oh, so marvelous. A small slice will hold your chocolate cravings, for a while ...

Chewy Apple Pecan Pie

¾   cup plain flour
¾   cup sugar
1½ teaspoons baking powder
1   egg, beaten

1   teaspoon vanilla
1   cup green apples, peeled and
    diced
½   cup pecans, chopped

Sift flour, sugar, and baking powder together. Mix in the well-beaten egg and vanilla. Stir in the apples and pecans. Bake in a greased pie pan (with no crust) at 300° for 1 hour.

First Prize Lemon Pie

1 cup sugar	1 tablespoon butter
½ cup plain flour	Rind of 1 lemon, grated
¼ teaspoon salt	Juice of 1 lemon
2 cups boiling water	1 8-inch baked and cooled pie
2 egg yolks, beaten	crust

Meringue:

2 egg whites, room temperature	2 tablespoons sugar

In a saucepan, mix sugar, flour, and salt; add boiling water and stir until dissolved. Stirring constantly, cook sugar mixture over medium heat until thickened. Add beaten egg yolks **very slowly** to the hot mixture; then cook on low for about 1 minute. Add butter, lemon rind, and lemon juice; stir until butter is melted and juice is blended. Cool lemon filling **completely** before pouring into the baked pie crust.

Meringue:

In an electric mixer, beat egg whites until very stiff and dry; then add sugar. Cover top of lemon filling in the pie crust with meringue, and bake at 400° for just long enough to turn meringue a light brown.

Many years ago, my grandmother was given this recipe by a friend who had won First Prize at the Fair. The only clue to just how old the recipe could be, is in the original wording—"Cook on the back of the range."

Pastry Made in Food Processor

½ cup cold margarine	¼ cup ice water
1⅓ cups plain flour	

Preheat oven to 425°. Cut margarine into several pieces and place with flour in food processor with steel blade; process until the consistency of corn meal. With processor running, pour in the ice water. The dough will form into a ball. Roll out dough on waxed paper, and place in a 9-inch pie pan. Bake at 425° for 12-15 minutes. The dough can be wrapped in plastic wrap and stored in the refrigerator for several days. Yield: 1 9-inch crust.

French Liqueur Pie

This recipe makes 2 pies. Prepare the day before serving.

½ gallon vanilla ice cream
1   cup pecans, chopped and
    toasted
Creme de menthe liqueur or
    syrup

2   chocolate cookie pie crusts
Toasted pecan halves to
    decorate top of pies

Soften ice cream enough to stir in the chopped pecans and creme de menthe to desired taste and color. Pour into the cookie crusts, and decorate the tops with the pecan halves. Cover with the plastic liners from the cookie crusts, and freeze overnight. Yield: 2 pies.

No slaving over this dessert. It's almost embarrassingly easy to make and, yet, always gets raves.

Chocolate Pecan Pie

This recipe makes 2 pies.

½ cup margarine, melted
1   cup sugar
1   cup light corn syrup
4   eggs, well beaten
2   tablespoons bourbon

¾ cup semisweet chocolate
    morsels
1¼ cups pecans, chopped
2   unbaked 9-inch pie crusts
Whipped cream (optional)

Preheat oven to 350°. Combine margarine, sugar, syrup, beaten eggs, bourbon, semisweet morsels, and pecans. Mix well; then pour into the unbaked pie crusts, dividing evenly. Bake at 350° for 40-45 minutes or until firm. Serve warm or cold topped with lightly sweetened whipped cream, if desired.

Old Fashioned Cobbler Made Easy

2	deep-dish pie crusts, unbaked	¾	cup water
1	quart fresh berries	¾	cup sugar
		¼	cup margarine, cut in slices

Preheat oven to 425°. Remove one of the pie crusts from the aluminum plate onto a sheet of waxed paper. Let thaw; then flatten, and slice into strips. In the remaining pie crust, make a layer of ½ of the berries; then add the water. Sprinkle evenly with ½ of the sugar, and distribute ½ of the margarine slices on top of the sugared berries. Place ½ of the pie crust strips in a lattice design on top. Repeat with a layer of berries, sugar, margarine, and finish with remaining pie crust strips in the lattice design. Place on a preheated cookie sheet. Cook in a preheated oven at 425° until the mixture bubbles; then reduce heat to 250°, and bake for 1½ hours.

Old Fashioned Chocolate Pie

1	cup sugar	1	tablespoon margarine
2	tablespoons cocoa	1	teaspoon vanilla
⅓	cup plain flour		Pinch of salt
2	cups boiling water		9-inch pie crust
2	eggs, separated		

In a saucepan, mix sugar, cocoa, and flour until well-blended. Add boiling water, mix, and cook over low heat until very thick. Allow to cool for 5 minutes; then slowly stir in the egg yolks. Beat well. Cook mixture on low for 1 minute, stirring. Add margarine, vanilla, and salt; blend well. Allow pie filling to cool completely. While filling is cooling, bake the pie crust according to package directions. Cool crust completely before filling. In an electric mixer, beat room temperature egg whites until stiff. Sweeten to taste. Pile the meringue on top of the chocolate pie. Bake at 325° until meringue is light brown.

French Cloud Chocolate Pie

Make the pie early in the day. Do not make the day before serving.

2 egg whites, room temperature	⅛ teaspoon salt
½ cup sugar	½ teaspoon vanilla
⅛ teaspoon cream of tartar	½ cup pecans, chopped

Filling:

4 ounces German sweet chocolate, broken in pieces	Sugar to taste
3 tablespoons water	1 teaspoon vanilla
1 pint whipping cream	Chocolate Leaves for garnish, if desired (see A Duke's Mixture)

Preheat oven to 300°. In an electric mixer, beat egg whites until very stiff; then add sugar, and blend well. Add cream of tartar, salt, and vanilla. By hand, fold in the pecans. Place in an 8-inch pie dish, covering the bottom and building up the sides to make a shell. Bake at 300° for 50-55 minutes. Cool completely before adding filling. To make the filling, use a double boiler over simmering water, melt the chocolate pieces, and add the water. Whip the cream, and sweeten to taste. Add vanilla, and the melted chocolate to whipped cream, and gently mix. Pour into the cooled shell, and refrigerate. Garnish with Chocolate Leaves (see A Duke's Mixture) or fresh fruit slices.

Ken's Fudge Pie

½ cup margarine
6 tablespoons cocoa
2 tablespoons vegetable oil
2 eggs, well-beaten

¼ cup plain flour
1 cup sugar
¾ cup pecans, chopped

Preheat oven to 350°. Melt margarine and cocoa; add oil. Beat eggs well; then stir in flour, sugar, and melted cocoa mixture. Beat until thoroughly blended; add pecans, and pour into a greased pie dish (no pie crust is needed). Bake at 350° for about 25 minutes or until the center of the pie tests done.

Sour Cream Pecan Pie

3 eggs
½ cup sour cream
½ cup corn syrup
1 teaspoon vanilla
1 cup sugar

¼ teaspoon salt
2 tablespoons margarine, melted
1¼ cups pecan halves
1 (9-inch) unbaked pie shell

Beat eggs well, and stir in sour cream. Add corn syrup, vanilla, sugar, salt, and margarine; blend well. Stir in the pecans; then pour into the unbaked pie shell. Bake at 400° for 30-35 minutes until pie is puffy and crust is lightly browned.

Basic Pastry

½ cup margarine
1⅓ cups plain flour

3 tablespoons ice water

Cut margarine into flour until it looks like corn meal. Sprinkle with ice water, and mix with a fork into a dough. Roll out on a floured surface. Yield: 1½ crusts.

Liz's Canadian Butter Tarts

1 cup plain flour, sifted	1 egg, slightly beaten
¾ cup margarine, softened and divided	¼ teaspoon salt
¼ cup powdered sugar, sifted	¼ cup currants or chopped raisins
¾ cup packed brown sugar	Sweetened whipped cream, if desired
¼ cup dark corn syrup	

Preheat oven to 350°. In an electric mixer, cream flour, ½ cup of the margarine, and powdered sugar. Divide the dough into 24 equal pieces. Press each piece into a mini muffin (1¾ × 1-inch) pan to form a "cup" on bottom and sides. Do not allow dough to extend above tops of pans. In a bowl, combine brown sugar and remaining ¼ cup of the margarine. Stir in corn syrup, egg, salt, and currants. Mix well. Spoon a scant table-spoonful of the mixture into each muffin "cup." Bake in a preheated oven at 350° for 20 minutes or until filling is set and crust is light brown. Cool muffins in the pans for 20 minutes. Remove from pans with the tip of a knife; cool on a wire rack. Top with the sweetened whipped cream, if desired. Yield: 24.

Recipe from a friend from British Columbia transplanted to the Canadian maritime province of Nova Scotia, with a couple of years' visits to Alabama and California. How's that for covering the good ole North American continent? Eh? Regardless of where she makes these tarts, they are delightful. The tarts can be individually wrapped in plastic wrap and placed in a covered container for freezing. Freeze no longer than 3 months. Unwrap and thaw at room temperature for 30 minutes.

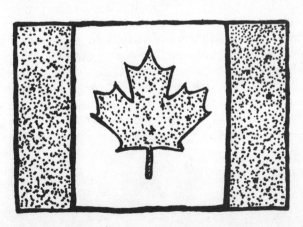

Piña Colada Cream Pie

1	envelope unflavored gelatin
¼	cup cold water
1	cup crushed pineapple
½	cup Coco Lopez cream of coconut
¼	cup light rum
½	cup whipping cream, whipped and divided
1	graham cracker crust
	Maraschino cherries, sliced

Soften gelatin in cold water. Heat pineapple in a 10-inch skillet to boiling; then stir in gelatin mixture until completely dissolved. Add Coco Lopez and rum. Chill in refrigerator or freezer until almost set (don't forget it!). Fold in ½ of the whipped cream, and pour into the pie shell. Refrigerate until firm; then garnish with remaining whipped cream, sweetened to taste, and the maraschino cherry slices.

Colonial Egg Custard Pie

3	eggs, well beaten
¾	cup sugar
¼	teaspoon salt
1	teaspoon vanilla
¼	teaspoon ground nutmeg
2	cups scalded milk
1	(9-inch) deep-dish unbaked pie crust
	Ground nutmeg for garnish

Preheat oven to 400°. Beat eggs and sugar together thoroughly. Add salt, vanilla, and the ¼ teaspoon nutmeg; mix well. Scald milk by placing milk into a saucepan rinsed in cold water, but not dried. Allow milk to heat until a film forms on top of milk. Test for the film by inserting a spoon into milk and slowly pulling it out. If a film comes up with the spoon, the milk is scalded. **Very slowly,** add the scalded milk to the egg mixture while stirring constantly. Pour mixture into the unbaked pie crust; sprinkle lightly with ground nutmeg. Bake in a preheated oven at 400° for 10 minutes. Reduce heat to 325°, and bake another 25 minutes or until a knife blade inserted in the center of the pie comes out clean. Remove from oven, and cool before serving.

Candies

Lou's Candied Spice Pecans

1   cup sugar
½   teaspoon cinnamon
⅓   cup milk

1½ cups pecan halves
½   teaspoon vanilla

Line a cookie sheet with waxed paper, and set aside to have ready when candy begins to harden. In a heavy saucepan, mix sugar and cinnamon. Stir in milk. Cook until the mixture reaches the soft ball stage. Remove from heat, and begin to beat the mixture. Add pecans and vanilla. Beat to coat the pecans. As soon as candy begins to harden, quickly pour onto the waxed paper, and separate the pecans to form individual pieces of candy.

Bourbon Balls

1   cup powdered sugar
1½ tablespoons cocoa
3   ounces bourbon or rum
2½ tablespoons corn syrup

1   pound vanilla wafers, crushed
1   cup nuts, chopped fine
Extra powdered sugar

Sift powdered sugar and cocoa into a bowl. Mix bourbon and corn syrup; then pour into the cocoa mixture. Blend well and stir in the crushed vanilla wafers and nuts. Mix all ingredients until thoroughly blended. Refrigerate for several hours for easier handling. Roll into small balls, and coat with powdered sugar. Allow several hours or overnight drying time before serving. Bourbon balls can be frozen. Yield: 36-40.

Oh, woe is my waist! Somehow, these tiny white goodies manage to leap into my hand, and feeling "duty-bound" not to waste . . . Ummmm.

Pecan Crunch Meringues

Make candies on a sunny day; moisture from rain will make candies sticky.

1 egg white, room temperature	⅛ teaspoon baking powder
¾ cup brown sugar, sifted	Pinch of salt
	2 cups small pecan halves

Preheat oven to 250°. In an electric mixer, beat egg white until stiff. Gradually beat in the sugar, baking powder, and salt; mix well. Stir in the pecan halves by hand. Drop each pecan, coated with the egg white mixture, onto a greased cookie sheet. Bake at 250° for 20 minutes. Turn oven off, and allow cookies to remain in the cooling oven for another 60 minutes. Do not open oven door after oven has been turned off. Store in an airtight container. Yield: about 125.

Very, very light—just a crunch of "sweet air".

Easy "Fudgy" Fudge

6 tablespoons margarine	1 pound powdered sugar, sifted
½ cup cocoa	
¼ teaspoon salt (do not omit)	4 tablespoons milk (all of the milk may not be needed)
1 teaspoon vanilla	1 cup nuts, chopped

In a double boiler over boiling water, melt margarine. Add cocoa, salt, and vanilla; mix well. Stir in the sifted sugar and blend. Add the milk a tablespoon at a time; use only enough milk to make mixture smooth. Add nuts and stir to coat. Pour quickly into a greased 5x9 loaf pan. If fudge gets too stiff to pour, place pan over boiling water again until softened, and finish pouring. Allow fudge to cool, then cut into small squares. Yield: 24.

So easy to make and never fails to get hard. None of that miserable, endless stirring and testing for a soft ball stage! The candy has an old fashioned "fudgy" texture; it is not creamy.

Divinity

Always make Divinity on a sunny day. The candy will not make properly when there is too much moisture in the air.

2½ cups sugar
⅛ teaspoon salt
½ cup white corn syrup
⅔ cup water

2 egg whites, allow to become room temperature, then beat very stiff
1 teaspoon vanilla
1½ cups pecans, chopped

Combine sugar, salt, corn syrup, and water; cook in a saucepan until the syrup reaches a soft ball stage (234°-240° on a candy thermometer). Remove ½ cup of the syrup, and continue cooking the remainder until it reaches the hard ball stage (about 266° on a candy thermometer). While the syrup is cooking to the hard ball stage, pour the ½ cup of syrup slowly over the stiffly beaten egg whites; beating constantly. Continue beating, and add the remaining syrup in small amounts when the hard ball stage is reached. Beat in vanilla and pecans, and continue beating until candy holds its shape when dropped from a spoon. Drop from a teaspoon onto waxed paper. Swirl each piece of candy with a spoon to form a peak. Work quickly since the candy hardens rapidly.

Tammy's Date Nut Balls

1 cup margarine
1 cup granulated sugar
1 pound dates, chopped
1 teaspoon vanilla
2 cups Rice Krispies

1 cup frozen coconut, thaw before measuring
1 cup nuts, chopped
Powdered sugar

In a skillet, cook margarine, granulated sugar, and dates very slowly for 10 minutes. Add remaining ingredients except powdered sugar, and let cool. Shape into balls, and roll in powdered sugar.

Frozen Desserts

Chocolate Rum Bombe

6 eggs, separated
½ gallon vanilla ice cream, slightly softened
6 ounces semisweet chocolate morsels

3 tablespoons rum
1 teaspoon vanilla
1 cup whipping cream

Garnish:
Chocolate Leaves (see A Duke's Mixture), fresh fruit slices, or fresh whole strawberries

Separate eggs, and let them come to room temperature. Freeze a 12-cup bowl until thoroughly cold; then slice the slightly soft ice cream block into ½-inch slices, and form a shell of ice cream in the chilled bowl, leaving the center hollow. Place the bowl in the freezer for 1 hour or until very firm. In the top of a double boiler, melt chocolate; add rum, and remove from heat. Very gradually add well-beaten egg yolks to chocolate, beating constantly; then beat in vanilla. In an electric mixer, whip cream, and sweeten to taste; set aside. Beat egg whites until stiff; then fold the egg whites and whipped cream into the chocolate mixture. Pour this mixture into the ice cream shell. Cover with waxed paper, then with aluminum foil. Place in the freezer for at least 4 hours. To serve, dip the bottom of the bowl into hot water for 30 seconds; then invert on a cold silver tray. Return to the freezer to allow any melted ice cream to harden. Decorate the top with the Chocolate Leaves, fruit slices, or strawberries, and cut like a pie to serve.

An elegant dessert with the flavors of ice cream and chocolate rum mousse.

Frozen Ice Cream Watermelon

½ gallon lime sherbet, slightly softened
6 ounces semisweet chocolate mini chips

½ gallon strawberry ice cream or raspberry sherbet, softened

In a large chilled oval or round bowl, make a shell of the lime sherbet, covering the bottom and sides of the bowl. Place the shell in the freezer and let the sherbet get firm. When lime sherbet is firm, stir the mini chips into the softened ice cream; then fill the sherbet shell with the mini chip mixture. Freeze until very firm. To serve, place bottom of the bowl into hot water for 30 seconds; then invert bowl onto a chilled silver tray. Return to the freezer to allow any melted sherbet to harden. Slice like a watermelon to serve.

An easy dessert that adds a "splash" of summer color to dinner's end.

Lemon Bisque

1 (13-ounce) can evaporated milk, chilled
¾ cup sugar

Juice of 3 large lemons or 6 tablespoons lemon juice
2 graham cracker crumb pie shells

Chill the evaporated milk overnight or for several hours; then whip in electric mixer until very frothy. Add sugar slowly, then lemon juice. Pour into pie shells. This can be garnished with thin lemon slices, sliced strawberries, or whole pecans. Cover and freeze overnight.

Most graham cracker pie shells have a clear plastic form that must be removed to use the shell. Save this form, and turn it upside-down over the filled pie shell, slipping the edges under the foil lip of the aluminum shell. You now have a cover and a convenient way to stack the pies in the freezer.

Frozen Chocolate Rocks Dessert

1 cup plain flour	1 cup pecans, chopped
¼ cup brown sugar	1 cup chocolate syrup
¼ cup oats	½ gallon vanilla ice cream, softened
½ cup margarine, melted	

Combine flour, brown sugar, oats, melted margarine, and pecans; mix well. Bake on a greased cookie sheet at 350° for 10 minutes. After 5 minutes of cooking time, break up the mixture on the cookie sheet to form the "rocks." Allow rocks to cool; then place ½ of them in the bottom of a greased square pan. Drizzle ½ cup of the chocolate syrup over the "rocks." Spread the ice cream over the syrup. Repeat layers of remaining "rocks" and chocolate syrup. Freeze until ice cream is very firm. Cut into squares to serve.

Amaretto Freeze

½ cup Amaretto	Whipped cream, sweetened
1 tablespoon brown sugar	Maraschino cherries, halved
1 quart vanilla ice cream, softened	

Combine Amaretto and brown sugar in the blender or food processor. Add ice cream, and blend until smooth. Pour into freezer-proof serving dishes; freeze. Just before serving, add a dollop of whipped cream topped with a cherry half. Serves 6.

Homemade Vanilla Ice Cream with Pineapple

1 quart milk	½ pint whipping cream
4 eggs	1 (20-ounce) can crushed
1 cup sugar, divided	pineapple in heavy syrup,
1 teaspoon vanilla	undrained and chilled

Rinse a 1½-quart saucepan in cold water; do not dry. Then add the milk, and cook over medium heat until a film forms on top of the milk. Test frequently with a fork, by dipping the fork into the milk and slowly pulling the fork back up. If a film comes up with the fork, then the milk is scalded. Scalding will occur before the milk boils. Set the scalded milk aside to cool. Beat the eggs with ½ cup of the sugar; then slowly add the cooled scalded milk to the eggs while stirring constantly. Pour this mixture into the top of a double boiler, cover, and cook over boiling water for 20 minutes; do not stir during this cooking. Remove from heat and allow to cool; add vanilla. Whip the cream in a chilled bowl, and add the remaining ½ cup sugar when cream is stiff. When the egg custard has cooled, fold in the whipped cream and the undrained pineapple. Freeze in an electric ice cream freezer.

Fresh Peach Sherbet

4 eggs, separated	1 (14-ounce) can sweetened
4 cups fresh peaches, peeled and diced very fine (about 5 large peaches)	condensed milk
	¼ cup reconstituted lemon juice
1 cup powdered sugar, sifted	

Separate eggs, and let them come to room temperature. Combine peaches and sugar; toss carefully to coat. In a large bowl, combine milk, lemon juice, and egg yolks; blend well. Stir in peaches. Beat the room-temperature egg whites until stiff, but not dry. Fold into peach mixture, and pour into a 9x13 dish. Cover with foil, and freeze for about 1½ to 2 hours or until a firm mush forms. Turn the mixture into a large, chilled bowl and break into pieces. Beat until fluffy, but not melted. Quickly return to the dish, and freeze. Allow to freeze for about 2 hours or until very firm. Yield: ½ gallon.

Just Desserts

French Roulage and Chocolate Roll

Both desserts are made with the same cake recipe, which does not contain flour. The cake fillings are different.

Cake:

6 eggs, separated and room temperature	1½ teaspoons vanilla
¾ cup sugar, divided	Pinch of salt
⅓ cup cocoa	Powdered sugar

Roulage filling:

2 cups whipping cream	1 cup nuts, chopped and toasted
⅓ cup powdered sugar	
1 teaspoon vanilla	

Chocolate Roll filling:

½ gallon vanilla ice cream	Powdered sugar
1 cup nuts, chopped and toasted	Whipped cream (optional)

Cake directions:

In a large electric mixer bowl, allow egg whites to come to room temperature. Grease the bottom of a 10½x15½-inch cookie sheet, and line it with waxed paper. Preheat the oven to 375°. Beat egg whites until soft peaks form; then slowly add ¼ cup of the sugar, and continue beating until stiff peaks form. In another bowl, beat egg yolks at high speed; add remaining ½ cup sugar, and beat for 4 minutes. Reduce speed to low to add the cocoa, vanilla, and salt. With a rubber spatula, fold cocoa mixture into the egg whites, and mix until just blended. Pour into the waxed-paper-lined baking pan, and bake at 375° for 15 minutes or until cake springs back when touched. Place a clean tea towel on a flat surface, and sift powdered sugar over the entire surface of the towel. When cake is done, turn the hot cake, cake side down, onto the sugared tea towel, and immediately peel the waxed paper off the bottom of the cake. Some of the cake may stick to the waxed paper, and the top may be a little ragged, but all of that surface will be filled and rolled inside. While cake is still hot, roll tea towel and cake together in jelly roll style, beginning at the narrow end of the cake. Allow cake to cool completely on a rack or place in the refrigerator with the seam side down.

(Continued next page)

French Roulage Filling Directions:

Whip cream; add sugar and vanilla until blended. Stir in the nuts, by hand. Refrigerate cream until ready to use. When cake is cooled, unroll and spread with ¾ of the filling; then roll again (without tea towel). Place on serving platter with seam side down. Place remaining filling in a fluffy line on top of the roll. Dust with powdered sugar. Refrigerate until serving time. Can be made a day in advance. Serves 10.

Chocolate Roll Directions:

Soften ice cream just enough to slice with a knife neatly. Slice enough ice cream, in ½ inch slices, to cover entire surface of the unrolled cake. Sprinkle with nuts and roll (without tea towel) jelly-roll style, beginning at the narrow end. Dust top of roll with powdered sugar and decorate with whipped cream and chopped nuts. Place in the freezer, seam side down, until ready to serve. Serves 10.

Bavarian Cream

This is a "Baby Sitter" recipe; you must give it your full attention to make it correctly. The taste is light and heavenly and very much worth your time.

2 envelopes plain gelatin	1 cup whipping cream,
½ cup cold water	whipped and refrigerated
3 cups milk	3 tablespoons cooking sherry
4 eggs, separated	1 package lady fingers, split
1 cup sugar	(optional)
⅛ teaspoon salt	

Can be made the day before serving. Soak gelatin in cold water. In a double boiler over boiling water, cook milk, beaten egg yolks, sugar, and salt to a thin custard stage. Remove from heat; immediately add softened gelatin and mix very well. Place custard in the refrigerator or in a large bowl of ice. Chill the custard just until it begins to thicken. (Do not let it get hard.) When slightly thickened, add whipped cream and stiffly beaten egg whites. Finally, add cooking sherry. Line serving bowl with the split lady fingers and pour custard mixture into the bowl, or use a pretty mold without the lady fingers. Refrigerate and let set. Serves 12.

Fabulous Boccone Dolce

4   egg whites, room
    temperature
¼   teaspoon cream of tartar
Scant ⅛ teaspoon salt
1⅓ cups sugar, divided
1   pint fresh strawberries

2   medium fresh peaches,
    peeled and sliced very thin
3   tablespoons water
6   ounces semisweet real
    chocolate morsels
2   cups whipping cream

Preheat oven to 250°. In an electric mixer, beat room temperature egg whites until very stiff, but not dry. Add cream of tartar and salt; then gradually beat in 1 cup of the sugar. Cut three 8-inch circles from waxed paper. Dot the edges of the waxed paper with solid shortening to hold paper flat on pans. Place 2 circles on a cookie sheet and the remaining circle on the bottom side of an 8-inch cake pan. Press edges of paper where shortening is located to firmly seat the waxed paper. Divide the meringue evenly between the 3 circles, and spread meringue to cover entire surface of waxed paper with a uniform thickness. Bake on the middle rack of the preheated oven at 250° for 25 to 30 minutes. Remove meringues from the oven, and carefully peel off the waxed paper. The meringues will still be pliable. Place meringues on a rack to cool.

Place mixer bowl, beaters, and the ⅓ cup sugar, to be used later to sweeten the whipped cream, into the refrigerator to chill thoroughly. Select about 5 or 6 of the best strawberries to reserve for garnishing. Slice remaining strawberries, and the peaches into a colander to allow any juice to drain away from the fruit.

In a small saucepan, bring the water to a boil; add semisweet morsels. Cover saucepan and remove from the heat; stir once to mix. Set aside to allow chocolate to melt. While chocolate is melting, whip the cream until stiff; then gradually beat in the remaining ⅓ cup of chilled sugar. The whipped cream needs to be stiff to hold its form in the dessert.

To assemble, place a meringue layer on a silver or crystal platter or cake stand. Stread the meringue with ½ of the chocolate. Top chocolate with a ½-inch layer of whipped cream. On top of the cream, arrange ½ of the thin peach slices in circles, and cover with ½ of the strawberry slices. Repeat the layers with another meringue, chocolate, whipped cream, peaches, and strawberries. Place the remaining meringue on top, and frost top with whipped cream. The sides can be frosted or left open for the fruit to show. Use the reserved whole strawberries to decorate the top. Refrigerate for at least 2 hours before serving. Serves 12. *Spectacularly beautiful dessert to delight the epicurean in all of us.*

220

Chocolate Lady Finger Dessert

Prepare 1 day before serving.

6   eggs, separated and room temperature
1   cup sugar, divided
4   squares unsweetened chocolate
1   teaspoon vanilla

Pinch of salt
18 lady fingers, split
½ pint whipping cream, whipped and sweetened with 3 tablespoons sugar

In an electric mixer, beat egg yolks on high speed for 4 minutes. Add ½ cup of the sugar, and beat another 1 minute. Melt chocolate in a double boiler; do not allow chocolate to cook. Allow melted chocolate to almost cool; then add chocolate to the egg yolks. Stir in vanilla and salt; mix well. Using the electric mixer with a fresh bowl and beaters, beat egg whites until stiff, but not dry. Add remaining ½ cup of the sugar. Carefully fold egg whites into chocolate mixture. Line bottom and sides of a 4-inch deep crystal bowl with the split lady fingers. Pour mixture over the lady fingers, and refrigerate for 24 hours. After the chocolate mixture has set up, frost the dessert with the whipped cream. Place remaining lady fingers, cut in half, into the top of the dessert (press them into whipped cream and chocolate mixture vertically). Keep dessert refrigerated until serving time. Serves 8-10.

Whipped Cream

½ pint heavy cream
3   tablespoons powdered sugar, unsifted

½ teaspoon vanilla

For best results for whipping cream to hold shape for several hours, pour the cream into a mixer bowl, and place the loose electric mixer beaters in the bowl. Refrigerate bowl, cream, and beaters until very cold. Also refrigerate the measured sugar and vanilla in separate bowls. Whip cream until stiff; add the chilled sugar and vanilla. Keep whipped cream refrigerated.

Bavarian Apple Torte

Crust:

½ cup margarine, softened
⅓ cup sugar

¼ teaspoon vanilla
1 cup plain flour, sifted

Filling:

8 ounces cream cheese
¼ cup sugar

1 egg, beaten
½ teaspoon vanilla

Topping:

4 green apples, peeled and sliced thin
⅓ cup sugar

½ teaspoon cinnamon
½ cup nuts, chopped

Preheat oven to 450°. To prepare crust, cream margarine, sugar, and vanilla in an electric mixer. Add flour, and mix well. Spread in the bottom, and up the sides of a greased 9-inch torte pan or deep round baking dish. To prepare filling, combine cream cheese, sugar, beaten egg, and vanilla until smooth. Spread over the crust. To prepare the topping, toss together the apples, sugar, cinnamon, and nuts; then spoon over the filling. Bake in the preheated 450° oven for 10 minutes; then reduce temperature to 400°, and continue baking for 25 minutes more. Cool torte before cutting.

Banana Flambé

Vanilla ice cream
½ cup rum
½ cup butter

½ cup brown sugar
6 bananas

Place a serving of ice cream in each of 6 compotes or on dessert plates. Keep ice cream servings frozen until serving time. In a saucepan, begin heating rum on low heat. In another saucepan or in a chafing dish, melt butter; then stir in the brown sugar until dissolved. Peel bananas, and slice in half lengthwise; then half each of those slices. Add bananas to the butter sauce and simmer for 5 minutes. Remove ice cream from freezer, and place banana slices and butter sauce over ice cream. Bring rum to a boil, and **carefully** ignite. Spoon flaming rum over the ice cream and bananas. Serves 6.

Chocolate Almond Crêpe Torte

6	ounces semisweet real chocolate morsels	1	teaspoon vanilla
½	cup margarine	8	cooked crêpes (see Crêpes)
¼	cup water	1	cup whipping cream, whipped and sweetened to taste
4	egg yolks, slightly beaten		
2	tablespoons powdered sugar	¼	cup sliced toasted almonds

In a small saucepan, slowly heat and blend the chocolate morsels, margarine, and water; cool slightly. Slowly stir in the beaten egg yolks, sugar, and vanilla. Refrigerate for about 1 hour until mixture is spreading consistency. Spread cooled crêpes with the chocolate mixture and stack. Spread the whipped cream over the top crêpe, and sprinkle with the almonds. Cut like a pie to serve. Refrigerate any unused portion. Serves 6-8.

True chocolate lovers will revel in this recipe. Double the recipe for a taller dessert, but remember, it's quite rich, and small wedges are an appropriate serving size. Be imaginative with the whipped cream on the top crêpe, and make a design accented with extra toasted almonds. Sinfully good!

Apple Crunch

6	medium green apples, peeled and sliced	¾	cup sugar
½	cup margarine	1	cup plain flour

Place the apple slices into a greased 2-quart baking dish. Melt the margarine; then stir in the sugar, and mix well. Add flour and mix again. Spread this thick mixture over the top of the apples as evenly as possible. Some small areas may not be totally covered. Bake at 350° for about 45 minutes or until apples are cooked and top is a light brown. Serves 4-6.

Beaux Arts Dessert

1 cup plain flour	16 ounces whipped topping, divided
½ cup margarine, melted	
1 cup nuts, chopped	3½ cups cold milk
8 ounces cream cheese, softened	2 (3¾-ounce) packages instant chocolate pudding mix
½ cup powdered sugar, sifted	1 teaspoon vanilla

Mix flour, margarine, and nuts. Place in a greased, flat, 2-quart baking dish. Bake at 350° until lightly browned, about 10 minutes. Allow to cool. In an electric mixer, blend the cream cheese, powdered sugar, and 1 cup of the whipped topping. Spread over the cooled crust. In a bowl, mix the milk, pudding mix, and vanilla. Spread over the cream cheese mixture. Refrigerate until chilled; then spread remaining 1 cup of whipped topping as the final layer. Refrigerate for several hours until well set. Cut into squares to serve.

If you like the cookie-type crust, try doubling the flour, margarine, and nuts to make a thicker crust for this light dessert.

Cherries Jubilee

Vanilla ice cream	1 tablespoon cornstarch
1 (17-ounce) can pitted bing cherries with liquid	4 tablespoons Triple Sec
	1 ounce brandy
4 tablespoons sugar	

Place a serving of ice cream in each of 4 compotes or on dessert plates. Freeze until serving time. In a saucepan, add cherry liquid, sugar, and cornstarch. Heat slowly, while stirring, until sauce is thickened; keep warm. Just before serving, place Triple Sec and brandy in a small saucepan over low heat. Add cherries to the cherry sauce to heat. Remove ice cream from freezer, and spoon the hot cherries and sauce over the ice cream. Bring the spirits to a boil and **carefully** ignite. Spoon the flaming spirits over the ice cream and cherries. Serves 4.

Cookie Strawberry Shortcake

1 pint fresh strawberries	1 (10-ounce) package Lorna
Sugar to taste	Doone cookies
½ pint whipping cream	

Wash and drain the strawberries. Slice strawberries into a bowl, and add sugar to taste; refrigerate. Whip cream in a cold bowl with cold electric mixer beaters; add sugar to taste. On individual dessert plates, place 4 cookies on each plate. Add 1 to 2 tablespoons sliced strawberries, and top with whipped cream; repeat the layers. Serve immediately to keep the cookies crisp. Serves 4.

Tia Maria's Top Banana

Fresh bananas, not overripe	Tia Maria Liqueur
Coffee ice cream	Whipped cream, sweetened

Slice peeled banana lengthwise. Cut the halves into 2 pieces each. Place 2 slices (½ banana) into an individual compote; add 2 scoops coffee ice cream. Drizzle Tia Maria Liqueur over ice cream, and top with a dollop of whipped cream.

Strawberries Romanoff

½ pint heavy cream, whipped	¼ cup Cointreau
1 pint vanilla ice cream,	¼ cup dark rum
slightly softened	2 quarts strawberries, hulled,
1 tablespoon fresh lemon juice	halved, sugared, and chilled

In a medium bowl, combine whipped cream with the softened ice cream. Add lemon juice, Cointreau, and rum. Pour over the strawberries and serve immediately. Serves 8.

Old Fashioned Baked Custard

4   eggs
½   cup sugar
¼   teaspoon salt

1   teaspoon vanilla
1   quart milk

Preheat oven to 300°. Beat together eggs, sugar, salt, and vanilla. Scald milk. (To scald milk, rinse a saucepan, 1½ quart or larger, in cold water; do not dry, and add milk. Cook, uncovered, at medium heat until a film forms on top of the milk. Test with a spoon or fork often for the film during the cooking. Film will form before boiling point.) Add the scalded milk to the egg mixture very slowly, beating constantly. Pour into greased baking dish or individual molds. Place in a pan of water. Bake at 300° for about 30-40 minutes. Test with a knife blade; it will come out "clean" if custard is set. Cool and refrigerate before serving.

This has the flavor of the "old days." Since it has no fillers, it is a delightful change. Don't let scalding the milk frighten you away. It's really quite simple. Once you dip the fork in the milk and pull it back out with a film on it—that's it!.

Nut Crisp

3   egg whites, room
     temperature
1   cup sugar
½   teaspoon baking powder

1   teaspoon vanilla
16 Ritz crackers, crushed
1   cup pecans, chopped
Ice cream

Preheat oven to 350°. In an electric mixer, beat egg whites very stiff. Combine sugar and baking powder; then gradually mix into the egg whites. Beat in the vanilla; then fold in the cracker crumbs and pecans. Spread into a 2-quart baking dish. Bake in a preheated oven at 350° for 20 minutes. Cool and cut into squares. Serve topped with ice cream. Serves 8-10.

First Lady Favorites

Nancy Reagan's Baja California Chicken

8　boned chicken breast halves
Seasoning salt and course
　ground pepper to taste
2　cloves garlic, crushed

4　tablespoons olive oil
4　tablespoons tarragon vinegar
⅔　cup dry sherry

Sprinkle chicken with seasoning salt and pepper. Crush garlic into oil in a skillet. Sauté chicken pieces until golden brown, turning frequently. Remove chicken from the skillet to a greased baking dish. Pour vinegar and sherry over chicken, and place in a 350° oven for 10 minutes or until breasts are tender.

Wonderful! A few well-chosen flavors combine for a fantastic treat for the palate.

Nancy Reagan's Pumpkin Pecan Pie

4　slightly beaten eggs
2　cups canned or mashed
　cooked pumpkin
1　cup sugar
½　cup dark corn syrup
1　teaspoon vanilla

½　teaspoon cinnamon
¼　teaspoon salt
1　unbaked deep dish 9-inch pie
　shell
1　cup chopped pecans

Combine ingredients except pecans. Pour into pie shell. Top with pecans. Bake at 350° for 40 to 45 minutes or until set.

Mrs. Reagan's two delicious recipes, used in the White House, represent very different areas of our nation — lower California and the South. Both are delightful taste sensations.

Betty Ford's Blu'Bana Bread

1 cup butter	1 teaspoon baking powder
2 cups sugar	½ teaspoon salt
4 eggs	2 cups fresh or frozen blueberries
2 teaspoons vanilla	
4 cups plain flour, divided	5 medium bananas, peeled and mashed
3 teaspoons allspice	
2 teaspoons soda	

Preheat oven to 325°. Grease and flour 2 loaf pans; set aside. In an electric mixer, cream butter and sugar; add eggs and vanilla. Beat on medium speed for 2 minutes. Measure flour, and sift; then re-measure flour by spooning lightly into cup. Reserve 2 tablespoons of flour, and set aside. Re-sift flour (minus the 2 tablespoons) with the allspice, soda, baking powder, and salt. Add flour mixture to creamed mixture; beat on medium speed until well-blended. Coat the blueberries with the reserved 2 tablespoons of flour. By hand, stir the coated blueberries and mashed bananas into the batter; mix well. Pour the batter into the 2 loaf pans, dividing it evenly. Bake in a preheated oven at 325° for approximately 50 minutes or until bread tests done. Yield: 2 loaves.

Mrs. Ford sent this grand sweet bread recipe with a letter saying: "The recipe is one that the Ford family has always enjoyed, and I hope that you will like it as well." I do, I do! As I am sure that all who try it will.

Claudia (Lady Bird) Johnson's Lace Cookies

½ cup plain flour	¼ cup brown sugar, firmly
½ cup frozen coconut, thawed	packed
before measuring	¼ cup margarine
¼ cup Karo syrup	½ teaspoon vanilla

Preheat oven to 325°. Mix flour with the coconut; set aside. In a saucepan, cook over medium heat, stirring constantly, Karo syrup, sugar, and margarine. Heat until well-blended and sugar is dissolved. Remove from heat, and stir in the vanilla. Gradually blend in the flour mixture. Drop by teaspoonfuls about 3 to 4 inches apart on an ungreased cookie sheet. Bake at 325° for 7 to 8 minutes. Allow cookies to cool before removing from the pan. Cookies should be very thin and crisp. As soon as cookies are cold, store in an airtight container to keep crisp. Yield: about 20 cookies.

Mrs. Johnson says "Just perfect for that special tea or brunch." Agreed, but don't stop there. They're so good for the family or as gifts for friends.

Mrs. Lyndon B. Johnson's Spoon Bread

1 scant cup plain corn meal	3 teaspoons baking powder
3 cups milk, divided	Butter the size of a walnut,
3 eggs, well beaten	melted
1 teaspoon salt	

In a saucepan, stir corn meal into 2 cups of the milk. Bring to a boil, making a mush. Remove from heat. Add remaining 1 cup of milk and the eggs. Stir in salt, baking powder, and melted butter. Bake in a greased casserole at 350° for 30 minutes.

Trail Foods

Occasionally in our lives, we arrive at times when a total change of pace, if only for brief intervals, gives us an appreciation of what we have been doing and a few thoughts about the future. I call it "time to clear the cobwebs." There are as many ways to accomplish this as there are individual imaginations. My husband, Joe, and I love nature, beautiful scenery, wildlife, and, particularly, mountains. We have discovered through our evolutionary process of first camping with tables, chairs, cots, etc. to our present-day backpacking hikes, that this is our way of "clearing our cobwebs." No telephones, no automobiles or airplanes, no everyday demands, no schedules—just a feeling of being a part of the mountains and all the beauty that they encompass. Perhaps, it's a latent pioneer spirit, both adventurous and exhilarating, that pushes us on to a glacier-fed cirque lake at 11,000 feet, where we are surrounded by jagged 13,000-foot peaks. Regardless, it's always an unforgettable experience.

Often back at home, I can mentally walk a particular trail that I've hiked only once, and call up vivid memories—a little snow storm, a huge moose walking through the willows along a mountain river, the young mountain goat kids playfully smacking their budding horns. Unathletic as I am, I must again load a pack on my back, tie on my less-than-ballerina-size boots, and walk at slower than a snail's pace up a high mountain trail.

The provisions given here are for a 6-day hiking trip in early October (snow is quite possible) for a man and woman in rugged, high terrain (up to 13,000 feet) with several days' elevation gain (a euphemism for "a tough climb"!). And despite it all, I still love the adventure!

Basic Daily Menu:

Breakfast	Lunch	Dinner
Tang	Summer Sausage	Soup
Instant Grits or Oatmeal	Cheese	Entrée
Cheddar Cheese	Crackers	Hot Chocolate
Bacon	Trail Mix	Coffee
Margarine	Lemonade	Trail Mix
Hot Chocolate		
Coffee		

I always pack a little extra food, usually an extra entrée and a couple of extra individual packages of grits and hot chocolate. The entrée, plus the foods you will probably have left over, will serve as a survival dinner in case of an emergency. The grits and hot chocolate are used as Southern Hospitality. Once while backpacking in the Great Smoky Mountains, we served hot grits with cheese and bacon, and a cup of hot chocolate to a pair of pre-med students from Notre Dame. They only had cold food, and our offer of a hot breakfast on that snowy October morning made Southerners of them! Remind me sometime to tell you about the young hiker we met in the Needle Mountains near Durango, Colorado.

Shopping List

1. Bacon – 3 (3-ounce) jars Hormel **real** bacon
2. Candies – hard candies in plastic wrappers. Select only the candies you like; do not get an assortment. Use 2-3 choices for a variety. These hard candies are the greatest source of energy for elevation gain that we have found. Plan on 10 candies per person per day of elevation gain. You'll each only need about 2 a day for other days.
3. Cheeses – 6 ounces sharp Cheddar
   3 ounces cream Havarti
   2 ounces Provolone
   3 ounces Swiss
   Use your own selections, of course, but keep in mind that all cheeses seem to taste milder in cold weather.
4. Coffee – 4 ounces freeze-dried
5. Crackers – 6 or 7 a day each. The large square Stone Ground Crackers made in Canada and Triscuits are 2 kinds of crackers that hold up well in a backpack.
6. Dinners – Mountain House freeze-dried dinners (have not tried other brands). One package serves as an entrée for the 2 of us. If 2 men are the hikers, perhaps you would need more. We have used all of these selections and found them good and enough for 2 people with other foods included in that meal. Selections include: Lasagna, Chicken and Rice, Sweet and Sour Pork, Shrimp Creole, Chicken Chop Suey, and Stroganoff. We found the Spaghetti too light an entrée for 2. When selecting your entrées, take care to alternate every other day with a non-tomato base entrée. Too much tomato-based food gets boring.
7. Grits or Oatmeal – Use individual packages that only require boiling water. Plan on 1 each per breakfast. If you use the grits, mix the cheese, margarine, and

bacon in with the grits. If you use the oatmeal, mix in the margarine, and have the cheese and bacon on the side.

8. Hot chocolate – 2 individual packages each per day
9. Lemonade – 4 ounces of the kind with sugar in it. Do not use a diet type; you need the sugar to get up the mountain!
10. Margarine – 3 ounces
11. Soups – Instant soup in individual packages requiring only boiling water and no cooking time. Plan on 1 each per dinner.
12. Summer sausage – ¾ pound, unsliced and in the casing to preserve it.
13. Tang – 7 ounces
14. Trail mix – ½ cup unsalted cashews
    1 cup unsalted, toasted pecan halves (toast dry, do not add margarine)
    1 cup of a mixture of raisins, chocolate chips, and M&M candies.
15. Heavy duty Ziploc bags – Buy both quart and gallon sizes. Do not use the sandwich bags that are light weight. Take a couple of unused, extra bags in your pack.

Tips and Notes:

Several days before the hike:

1. Package candies in Ziploc bag. Do not remove the plastic wrappers. Be sure to pack out even this little bit of plastic when the candy is gone.
2. Package loose coffee in Ziploc bag.
3. Place a wide, heavy-duty rubber band around one freeze-dried dinner package to have handy at cooking time. Use it to close the opening after adding water to rehydrate the dinner. Place the closed package in a pot with a small amount of boiling water, and cover with a lid. This method will keep the dinner hot as it rehydrates.
4. Place unopened grits or oatmeal packages in Ziploc bags.
5. Place unopened hot chocolate packages in Ziploc bags.
6. Package loose lemonade mix in a Ziploc bag.
7. Package unopened soups in a Ziploc bag.
8. Package loose Tang in a Ziploc bag.
9. Salt and pepper in small airtight containers.

Night before beginning hike:

1. Remove bacon from jars, and place in 2 quart-size bags. Refrigerate until departure time.
2. Keep cheeses in original wrappers, and place in Ziploc bags. Refrigerate until departure time.
3. Package crackers in 2 Ziploc bags. Carefully squeeze all the air out of the bag by leaving a tiny hole unsealed, and gently pressing the air out; then seal the hole. Fold excess plastic around the crackers, and place a rubber band around the whole package. This will prevent the crackers from moving inside the Ziploc bag.
4. Place margarine in a plastic food tube if the weather will be warm or hot. Place it in a Ziploc bag if weather will be cold. Refrigerate until departure time.
5. Package summer sausage in it's casing in a Ziploc bag. Refrigerate until departure time.
6. Make up your trail mix; packaging the nuts separately from the candy and raisins.
7. Take extra Ziploc bags.

A Special Note: Please pack out every scrap of evidence that you have been on the trail. Leave behind only a part of your spirit.

A Duke's Mixture

Ann's Homemade Mayonnaise

5   egg yolks, chilled
Juice of 3 large lemons, chilled
4   cups Wesson oil, chilled

2   teaspoons ice water
Salt to taste

Chill an electric mixer bowl and the beater blades. When all ingredients and utensils are chilled, beat egg yolks on high speed for 4 minutes. Add juice of 1 lemon; beat 1 more minute. Slowly, begin to add oil, pouring into the bowl with mixer on high speed. When mixture begins to thicken, add juice of another lemon. Keep sides of mixer bowl scraped with a rubber spatula. Continue to beat on high speed, alternating a very slow stream of oil and the remaining lemon juice. Beat for another 4 minutes; then beat in the ice water. Continue beating for 2 minutes; add salt to taste. Beat for another 2 minutes. Pour into chilled glass jars, and cap. Refrigerate. Yield: 1 quart plus.

Once you've tasted this marvelous "lemonnaise," it could be very difficult to go back to "store bought."

Chocolate Leaves

Real chocolate semisweet
  morsels

Freshly picked leaves, with
  stems

Select leaf size according to the dessert to be decorated. A firm, non-poisonous leaf such as Chinese holly or camellia works well; ivy leaves can also be used. According to the number of leaves to be made, melt semisweet morsels in a double boiler over simmering hot water. While chocolate is slowly melting, wash leaves thoroughly with soap and water. Dry each leaf completely. Line a cookie sheet with waxed paper and place near the chocolate. Hold the dry leaf by the stem, and spread melted chocolate on the **underside** of the leaf. Make chocolate thick to give strength, but avoid getting chocolate on the edges or front of leaf. Place chocolate-coated leaves on the waxed paper, and freeze until the chocolate is very firm. Remove leaves, one at a time, from the freezer. Hold by the stem, and gently peel the real leaf away from the chocolate leaf. Dip fingers into ice water to work with the chocolate. Immediately, return leaves to the freezer until ready to use.

Sylvia's Overnight Pickles

3 medium cucumbers	1 teaspoon dill weed
1 teaspoon mustard seed	1 tablespoon salt
1 teaspoon celery seed	White vinegar
1 teaspoon whole black pepper	

Peel cucumbers, and slice lengthwise into quarters or eights. Place the cucumber spears into salted water for several hours. Drain cucumbers, and place into a large glass saucepan. Add mustard seed, celery seed, pepper, dill weed, and salt. Add enough vinegar to the suacepan to cover the cucumbers. Bring cucumbers and vinegar to a boil; remove from heat, and cool. Cover and refrigerate overnight. The next morning, drain vinegar into a saucepan and bring to a boil. Pour the boiling vinegar over the cucumbers. Cool and refrigerate for 4-6 hours before serving.

My husband asked for this recipe at his aunt's 85th birthday celebration in Memphis, Tennessee. It was her grandmother's recipe — so it does date back! Very easy to prepare and great for the impatient, like me, who have difficulty waiting for things to pickle.

Cream Sauce

(Also called Bechamel or White Sauce)

2 tablespoons margarine or butter	1 cup milk
2 tablespoons plain flour	Salt to taste

In a skillet, melt the margarine, and stir in flour until smooth. Stirring constantly, gradually add milk, keeping the sauce smooth. Cook over medium heat, while stirring, until thickened; add salt to taste.

Cheese can be added to the cream sauce to change the flavor entirely. Use ½ to 1 cup of Cheddar, Swiss, Monterey Jack, or Gruyère for the effect you want. For Parmesan cheese, usually ¼ to ½ cup is sufficient. Many, many other flavors can be added to this very basic sauce.

Children's Thanksgiving Turkey (non-edible)

1   large unblemished apple
Round toothpicks

Raisins
1   large green stuffed olive

Clean the apple, and put a drop of vegetable oil on it to polish and make shiny. Place 2 toothpicks 1 inch apart on the narrower side of the apple. Place 1 toothpick on the back of the apple to balance the apple, allowing it to stand alone on toothpick "legs." Thread raisins onto 12-16 toothpicks, filling the toothpicks except for a small tip to pierce the apple. Arrange the raisin toothpicks in 2 rows fanned out and stuck into the back side of the apple to form the "turkey's feathers." Place 1 toothpick deep into the front of the apple to give him a "neck." Stick a large olive on his "neck," and gently pull the pimento out to give him a "gobbler."

Children love to make these on Thanksgiving day to place on the table as decoration. It gives them the feeling of having participated in the Pilgrims' feast.

Elephant Stew

1   medium-size elephant
2   rabbits

Salt and pepper

Cut the elephant into bite-size pieces. This should take about 2 months. Salt and pepper; then add enough brown gravy to cover. Cook over a kerosene fire for about 4 weeks at 465°. This dish will serve 3,800 people. If more guests arrive unexpectedly, add the 2 rabbits. Do this only if necessary, since some people do not like hare in their stew!!

Recipe still untested, since elephant season has not yet opened in Alabama.

Orange Pyramid Table Centerpiece

This is a non-edible recipe.

Medium-size oranges
2½ cups sugar
½ cup light Karo syrup

½ cup water
2 teaspoons cream of tartar

Make pyramid on a glass or silver platter with a small lip. Select enough fresh, firm, unblemished oranges to make a pyramid to fit your table (use at least 5 oranges for the base). Secure the oranges to each other with toothpicks, and build up to one orange on the top. When pyramid is firmly set-up on its platter, begin making the glaze. Be prepared to work quickly when the candy glaze reaches the hard-crack stage. In a medium-size, heavy saucepan, cook the sugar, syrup, water, and cream of tartar to the hard-crack stage on a candy thermometer. Being very careful because of the candy temperature, and using a large spoon, drizzle the candy glaze over the pyramid, letting it course down the sides from the top orange.

The Orange Pyramid makes an unusual and lovely centerpiece. Add greenery or flowers to suit the occasion. Chinese Holly with berries for Christmas, small daisies or mums, polished ivy leaves, Bells of Ireland — use your imagination. The Pyramid will last about 3 or 4 days, taking on a frosted appearance as time passes.

Homemade Mustard

Microwave recipe.

5 tablespoons dry mustard
½ cup sugar
½ teaspoon salt
2 tablespoons plain flour

1 cup milk
1 egg yolk
½ cup vinegar

Sift mustard, sugar, salt, and flour together. Stir in the milk, egg yolk, and vinegar; mix well. Cook in a glass 1-quart covered dish in the microwave on full power until thick, about 6 minutes. Pour into jars, and cap when cooled. Refrigerate to store.

Index

Index

Index

Index

Index

Index

Index

Index

Index

Index

Index

Vermicelli and Cheese, Genia's
  Baked, 148
Vermicelli Carbonara, 112
Vermicelli Toss, 150
Vichyssoise, Marvelous Hot, 50

W

Waffles, Buttermilk, 167
Watermelon, Spiked, 43
Weiners, Creole, 70
West Indies Salad, 57
Whipped Cream, 221
White Sauce, 237
Whole Smoked Turkey, 106
Wild Rice, 90
Williamsburg Cranberry Pecan
  Muffins, 170

Won Tons, 20

Y

Yeast Breads
  Angel Biscuits, 163
  Danish Pinwheel Rolls, 168
  Frances's Old Fashioned
    Homemade Rolls, 162
Yellow Layer Cake, 188

Z

Zucchini and Onion Crêpe
  Tower, Dawns's, 160

GENE WESTBROOK PUBLICATIONS
P.O. Box 869
Millbrook, Alabama 36054

Please send me_____copies of **THE MAGNOLIA COLLECTION**
(Includes Postage and Handling)   @ $15.99 each_____
(Or 3 for $41.85 plus $4.14 postage)   _____
Alabama residents add 4% sales tax   @   .56 each_____
Gift Wrap   @ · 1.00 each_____
                                        Total Enclosed_____

Print Name_____
Address_____
City_____State_____Zip_____
Checks to: GENE WESTBROOK PUBLICATIONS, INC. or Charge to:
Visa_____MC_____Acct.#_____
Print Name_____
Exp. Date_____Signature_____
TOLL FREE ORDER: 1-800-536-5407

- -

GENE WESTBROOK PUBLICATIONS
· P.O. Box 869
Millbrook, Alabama 36054

Please send me_____copies of **THE MAGNOLIA COLLECTION**
(Includes Postage and Handling)   @ $15.99 each_____
(Or 3 for $41.85 plus $4.14 postage)   _____
Alabama residents add 4% sales tax   @   .56 each_____
Gift Wrap   @   1.00 each_____
                                        Total Enclosed_____

Print Name_____
Address_____
City_____State_____Zip_____
Checks to: GENE WESTBROOK PUBLICATIONS, INC. or Charge to:
Visa_____MC_____Acct.#_____
Print Name_____
Exp. Date_____Signature_____
TOLL FREE ORDER: 1-800-536-5407

- -

GENE WESTBROOK PUBLICATIONS
P.O. Box 869
Millbrook, Alabama 36054

Please send me_____copies of **THE MAGNOLIA COLLECTION**
(Includes Postage and Handling)   @ $15.99 each_____
(Or 3 for $41.85 plus $4.14 postage)   _____
Alabama residents add 4% sales tax   @   .56 each_____
Gift Wrap   @   1.00 each_____
                                        Total Enclosed_____

Print Name_____
Address_____
City_____State_____Zip_____
Checks to: GENE WESTBROOK PUBLICATIONS, INC. or Charge to:
Visa_____MC_____Acct.#_____
Print Name_____
Exp. Date_____Signature_____
TOLL FREE ORDER: 1-800-536-5407